Riana,

MW00721008

Riana,

EASY CHINESE

Appetizers and Family Dishes

Tomiteru Shu

PUBLISHER REPRESENTATIVE OFFICE

UNITED STATES: Prime Communication System

    P. O. BOX 456 Shaw Island, WA 98286

AUTHOR'S SALES AGENCY: A. K. HARANO COMPANY

    P. O. BOX 1022 Edmonds, WA 98020

    Phone: (206)774-5490 FAX: (206)774-5490

    D & BH ENTERPRISE

    94-443 Kahuanani Street, Waipahu, HI 96797

    Phone: (808)671-6041

OVERSEAS DISTRIBUTORS

UNITED STATES:	JP TRADING, INC.
	300 Industrial Way
	Brisbane, Calif. 94005
	Phone: (415)468-0775, 0776 Fax: (415)469-8038
MEXICO:	Publicaciones Sayrols, S. A. de C. V.
COLOMBIA:	Jorge E. Morales & CIA. LTDA.
TAIWAN:	Formosan Magazine Press, Ltd.
HONG KONG:	Apollo Book Company, Ltd.
THAILAND:	Central Department Store Ltd.
SINGAPORE:	MPH DISTRIBUTORS (S) PTE, LTD.
MALAYSIA:	MPH DISTRIBUTORS SDN, BHD.
PHILIPPINES:	National Book Store, Inc.
KOREA:	Tongjin Chulpan Muyeok Co., Ltd.
INDONESIA:	C. V. TOKO BUKU "MENTENG"
INDIA:	Dani Book Land, Bombay 14
AUSTRALIA:	BOOKWISE INTERNATIONAL
GUAM, SIPAN AND MICRONESIAN ISLANDS:	FUJIWARA'S SALES & SERVICE
CANADA:	MILESTONE PUBLICATIONS
U. S.A.:	MASA T. & ASSOCIATES

Original Copyright © 1997 by Tomiteru Shu and Kazuo Mizutani

World rights reserved by JOIE, INC. 1-8-3, Hirakawa-cho, Chiyoda-ku, Tokyo 102 Japan;   printed in japan.

No part of this book or portions there of may be reproduced in any form or by any means including electronic retrieval systems without prior written approval from the author or publisher.

ISBN4-915831-78-7

INTRODUCTION

Chinese dishes can be classified into several kinds, such as; Peking, Shang Hai, and Szechwan. The recipes I introduce here are taken from the Cantonese style, which have been passed down to me from my father, a Chinese cook.

Of the various types of Chinese cooking, Cantonese has a lighter taste and uses less oil compared to those of other districts. I suppose this is the reason for its popularity, not only in China and Japan, but throughout the world. Another characteristic is its ample use of seafood and vegetables. Even in meat dishes you'll often see a large amount of vegetable, which offers a good nutritional balance.

This book shows you everyday dishes to go with wine or rice, one-bowl meals over noodles and rice, dim sum that can be served as a snack or meal, and refreshing desserts. I focused on supplying the recipes that can be prepared as easily as possible with professional results. Try a single dish or plan a full course meal from appetizers to dessert. Since Chinese dishes are meant for sharing with friends, they will make a heartwarming party menu as well. I have included special suggestions with each recipe that will guarantee success. A little attention goes a long way.

Some secret techniques are given to keep the food light and non-oily. I hear some people say Chinese dishes are greasy and I, myself, don't like oily food. Therefore, I stir-fry vegetables quickly and then boil them in hot water to remove any excess oiliness. This way the food will have less oil and fewer calories as well.

Another point is to season meats and thawed seafood before cooking them. It enhances not only the flavor of the meat or fish itself, but, also the whole dish because its natural flavor is sealed in and cooking can continue when other ingredients are added. Another advantage is that you can hold the intake of salt and sugar to minimum this way, because seasonings added during cooking do not work effectively and you may want to use more and more as you taste test while you are cooking.

Don't hesitate to try substitutes when the ingredients in recipes are not available. Use any similar food or one that is in season. Don't think you can't make a particular dish because you don't have the exact thing. I, myself, have adapted what I learned to new ingredients or combinations of my own.

It is important to check the taste and adjust it to your liking. Also try some of the unique sauces, such as, oyster, sa cha, and XO, which give Chinese cooking special flavors. They will make a big difference to your dish. The most important rule of all is to follow the basics of cooking introduced in this book. Even a professional cook will follow the steps provided in order to serve a really good dish. Lastly, when you cook, always say to yourself, "I want them to be happy", just like I do when I work in the kitchen of my restaurant. This is essential.

Well, enjoy cooking and make everyone happy. Creating a pleasant mood will make your food even more delicious!

Tomiteru Shu

BASIC COOKING INFORMATION

Today many areas of the world use the metric system and more will follow in the future. The following conversion tables are intented as a guide to help you.

General points of information that may prove valuable or of interest:

1 cup is equivalent to 240ml in our recipes: (American cup measurement)

1 American cup＝240ml＝8 American fl oz

1 British cup＝200ml＝7 British fl oz

1 Japanese cup＝200ml

1 tablespoon＝15ml　　　　1 teaspoon＝5ml

TABLES CONVERTING FROM U.S. CUSTOMARY SYSTEM TO METRICS

Liquid Measures

U.S. Customary system	oz	g	ml
¹⁄₁₆ cup＝ 1T	½ oz	14g	15ml
¼ cup＝ 4T	2 oz	60g	59ml
½ cup＝ 8T	4 oz	115g	118ml
1 cup＝16T	8 oz	225g	236ml
1¾ cups	14 oz	400g	414ml
2 cups＝1 pint	16 oz	450g	473ml
3 cups	24 oz	685g	710ml
4 cups	32 oz	900g	946ml

Liquid Measures

Japanese system	oz	ml
⅛ cup	⅞ oz	25ml
¼ cup	1¾ oz	50ml
½ cup	3½ oz	100ml
1 cup	7 oz	200ml
1½ cups	10½ oz	300ml
2 cups	14 oz	400ml
3 cups	21 oz	600ml
4 cups	28 oz	800ml

Weights   grams×0.035＝ounces   ounces×28.35＝grams

ounces to grams*	grams to ounces
¼ oz＝ 7g	1g＝0.035 oz
½ oz＝ 14g	5g＝ ⅙ oz
1 oz＝ 30g	10g＝ ⅓ oz
2 oz＝ 60g	28g＝ 1 oz
4 oz＝115g	100g＝ 3½ oz
6 oz＝170g	200g＝ 7 oz
8 oz＝225g	500g＝ 18 oz
16 oz＝450g	1000g＝ 35 oz

＊Equivalent

Linear Measures   inches×2.54＝centimeters   centimeters×0.39＝inches   in＝inch(es)   cm＝centimeter(s)

inches to centimeters	centimeters to inches*
½ in ＝ 1.27 cm	1 cm＝ ⅜ in
1 in ＝ 2.54 cm	2 cm＝ ¾ in
2 in ＝ 5.08 cm	3 cm＝1⅛ in
4 in ＝10.16 cm	4 cm＝1½ in
5 in ＝12.7 cm	5 cm＝ 2 in
10 in ＝25.4 cm	10 cm＝ 4 in
15 in ＝38.1 cm	15 cm＝5¾ in
20 in ＝50.8 cm	20 cm＝ 8 in

The water boiling temperature given is at sea level.

Conversion factors:

$$C=(F-32)\times\frac{5}{9}$$

$$F=\frac{C\times9}{5}+32$$

C＝Celsius   F＝Fahrenheit

Temperature

Fahrenheit (F) to Celsius (C)		Celsius (C) to Fahrenheit (F)	
freezer storage	−10°F＝−23.3°C	freezer storage	−20°C＝−4°F
	0°F＝−17.7°C		−10°C＝14°F
water freezes	32°F＝ 0 °C	water freezes	0°C＝32°F
	68°F＝ 20 °C		10°C＝50°F
	100°F＝37.7°C		50°C＝122°F
water boils	212°F＝100 °C	water boils	100°C＝212°F
	300°F＝148.8°C		150°C＝302°F
	400°F＝204.4°C		200°C＝392°F

Deep-Frying Oil Temperatures

300°F−330°F(150°C−165°C)＝	low
340°F−350°F(170°C−175°C)＝	moderate
350°F−360°F(175°C−180°C)＝	high

Oven Temperatures

250°F−350°F(120°C−175°C)＝	low or cool
350°F−400°F(175°C−204°C)＝	moderate or medium
400°F−450°F(204°C−230°C)＝	hot
450°F−500°F(230°C−260°C)＝	very hot

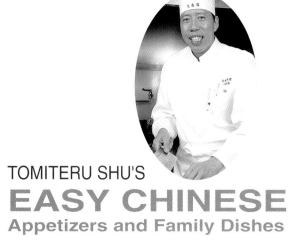

TOMITERU SHU'S
EASY CHINESE
Appetizers and Family Dishes

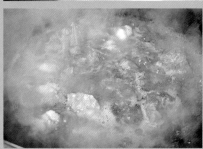

Shu-san's advice

Techniques of Chinese Cooking ······8

Family Dishes and appetizers

My Favorite Sauces ·····················38

You'll be glad you had it !
Chinese Seasonings and Utensils ··· 72

Rice, Noodles and Soups

Dim Sum and Desserts

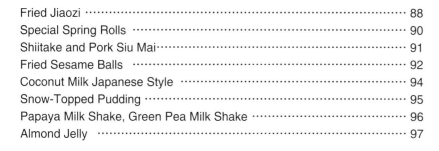

● Although most recipes in this book are for four servings, some pictures present one serving only.

● Measuring standards in this book are: 1 tablespoon: 15ml, 1 teaspoon: 5ml, 1 cup: 200ml

● "Dissoived cornstarch" is a mixture of cornstarch and water in a ratio of 1 : 2. Always stir before adding to sauce.

Useful Signs

Following signs on the direction pages indicate useful cooking tips :

HELPFUL HINT	CHEF'S SECRET	PROBLEMS TO AVOID

★ Important for success.

★ Shu-san's advice from a proffesional point of view.

★ Avoid mistakes by knowing possible troubles.

I'll show you how!!

Shu-san's Advice

Techniques of
Chinese Cooking

Chinese dishes cooked at home can become oily in texture. Each ingredient might not absorb the seasonings well. You may think it is too much trouble to blanch each food in hot oil... Shu has solved these problems, using efficient methods and new ideas. First, learn the basics below. These are a must to assure you deep flavor and a wide repertoire.

● Heat the wok well

When stir-frying, it is essential to preheat the wok until smoking hot. If this process is neglected, the ingredients will taste oily or scorch on the bottom of pan. When the wok is hot enough, pour in more oil than necessary and remove at once. Add required amount of oil to the hot wok coated with oil. Use this procedure when deep-frying as well.

● Check the taste

Do not forget to check the taste since the amount of seasonings will vary greatly depending on the ingredients and the diners' palates. Adjust the seasonings of the recipe accordingly, especially when using a mixture. Salad dressings and dipping sauces need tasting as well.

Garlic & Ginger: These two are essential for Chinese cooking. It is advisable to mince the same amount of each, sprinkle with oil and refrigerate in an air-tight container.

Common Basics

● Set all the seasonings near to hand

Searching for spice bottles and openig cans while stir-frying? Never in Chinese cooking. The taste will depend on the efficient adding of all the necessary seasonings. So set them in a place you can reach easily.

Preliminary Seasoning

Meats and seafood that are lightly seasoned prior to cooking will not only give deeper flavor but save salt snd sugar allowance to be used later. Especially effective in stir-frying dishes that require very short cooking time.

Chicken: Mix a little of each of the following through the meat: salt, MSG, pepper, rice wine, sesame oil, beaten egg, cornstarch, and vegetable oil. Finally coat with vegetable oil so the chicken pieces will separate easily when cooked.

Pork: Mix a little of each of the following through the meat : salt, MSG, pepper, rice wine, soy sauce, sesame oil, beaten egg, cornstarch, and vegetable oil. The peculiar smell of pork will turn flavorful by adding soy sauce.

Beef: Mix a little of the following through the meat, salt, sugar, MSG, pepper, rice wine, soy sauce or tamari soy sauce, baking soda, water, sesame oil, beaten egg, cornstarch, and vegetable oil. Chinese soy sauce adds a rich flavor.

Seafood: If using frozen fish or shellfish, add the following: salt, MSG, pepper, rice wine, sesame oil, egg white, baking soda, cornstarch, salad oil. Baking soda gives a pleasant resilience to seafood. Use only egg white as whole egg spoils the light color of seafood.

Blanching is the key to a healthy dish

In Chinese cooking, ingredients are often precooked by being deep-fried briefly in hot oil to seal in the flavors, but this is both time and oil consuming. The ideal method for home cooking is to stir-fry quickly in a small amount of oil, add boiling water and then discard the water. This way the flavors are reserved while the oil is removed.

Preheat wok. Add oil and quickly stir-fry.

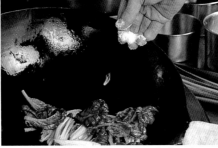

For greens, add a pinch of salt to retain the color.

Pour hot water and boil lightly, then strain.

Finishing touches

To finish stir-fry cooking, professionals add sesame oil or soy sauce in order to enhance the flavor. Even for seafood dishes which are usually seasoned only with salt, soy sauce sprinkled from the sides of wok gives a richer flavor. Sesame oil can be also used to soften the sharpness of hot bean paste. Add more sesame oil for those who prefer a milder taste.

Seal in the flavor

When deep-frying or stir-frying, it is essential to coat the ingredients with cornstarch before cooking. A thin coat of cornstarch seals in the flavor while cooking.

Appetizers & Family Dishes

No more "What am I going to cook today ?" Quickly stir-fried, braised, or steamed, each Chinese dish introduced here is a well-balanced combination of vegetables and meat, or fish, that will please any palate.

Ingredients   4 servings

500g(16oz) chicken legs
PRELIMINARY SEASONING
  2/3 teaspoon salt
  Pinch MSG
  Pinch Szechwan pepper (whole
    or powder)
MARINADE
  3 cups water
  5cm (2") green onion
  1 small fresh ginger root
  2 teaspoons salt
  1 tablespoon rice wine
  Pinch MSG

Pinch pepper
Dash sesame oil
1/2 stalk green onion
1 small cucumber
1 medium tomato
DRESSING
  1 teaspoon hot bean paste
  1 tablespoon rice vinegar
  1 tablespoon soy sauce
  1 tablespoon rice wine
  1 teaspoon sesame oil
  Pinch MSG
  Pinch sugar

Tender and juicy steamed chicken with
appetizing hot and spicy dressing

STEAMED
CHICKEN SALAD

HELPFUL HINT

★ When chicken is fully
cooked, cover and let stand
for a while. This way the
meat will stay soft and
fluffy.

 Directions

COOK CHICKEN

❶ Sprinkle chicken with salt and MSG and rub in well.
Then rub on Szechwan pepper and set aside for about
30 minutes (A).

❷ Place chicken in a hot steamer and steam for about 25
minutes. Cook until no blood comes out when a
bamboo skewer is inserted and removed (B).

❸ In a small saucepan, bring water to the boil. Crush
green onion and ginger using the back of a cleaver and
then cut into pieces ; and add to the boiling water. Add
remaining condiments.

❹ Place chicken, skin side down, marinate at least 1 hour.

CUT VEGETABLES

❺ Remove bones from chicken and cut into bite-size
pieces (C).

❻ Cut green onion into 1cm (3/8") diagonal slices. Slice
cucumber diagonally into 2cm (3/4") lengths and halve
lengthwise. Cut tomato into wedges, then halve. (D)

MIX WITH DRESSING

❼ Combine dressing ingredients (E).

❽ Toss chicken and vegetables with dressing (F).

● Ingredients ● 4 servings

1/2 tablespoon Chinese wolfberries

1 tablespoon rice wine

200g(7 oz) scallops

1/2 stalk green onion

Fresh coriander

Dash soy sauce

> If using frozen scallops, marinate them in a mixture of 1/2 teaspoon salt, pinch each MSG and pepper, 1 teaspoon rice wine, dash sesame oil, 1/2 tablespoon egg white, 1 teaspoon baking soda, 1 teaspoon corn-starch, and 1 teaspoon vegetable oil.

Scallops steamed in wine become very soft but chewy. Enhanced with green onion and coriander, this dish is recommended as an appetizer.

SCALLOPS STEAMED WITH CHINESE WOLFBERRIES

● Directions ●

PREPARE INGREDIENTS

❶ In a bowl, place Chinese wolfberries and pour over rice wine; soak until soft (A).

❷ Slice scallops into 2 to 3 rounds (B).

❸ Cut green onion into 6-7cm(2 1/2") lengths. Halve lengthwise and then shred; soak in cold water.

STEAM

❹ Preheat a steamer. In an heat proof dish place scallop slices and softened Chinese wolfberries. Pour over soaking water and put in a boiling steamer. Steam about 5 minutes (C).

❺ Arrange them on a serving plate and top with drained green onion and snipped coriander leaves. Pour over soy sauce just before serving.

HELPFUL HINT

★ Chinese wolfberries will look brighter in color if soaked in rice wine rather than water.

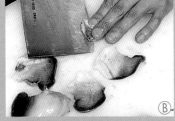

PREPARE SURF CLAMS

❶ Remove the filaments and pleated film from surf clams (A).

❷ Holding a cleaver horizontally, cut the flesh in half, and remove entrails. (B)

❸ In a wok bring water to the boil, and cook the shellfish and the filaments; drain (C).

❹ Remove black skin at the edges. Wash off any sand in syphon, and drain. Cut into bite-size pieces.

COAT WITH DRESSING

❺ In a bowl add dressing ingredients and mix well (D).

❻ Combine surf clams and dressing (E).

ARRANGE ON A PLATE

❼ Lay shiso leaves and center the clams. Garnish with sliced pepper and half moons of lemon.

CHEF'S SECRET

★ It is better to remove the "pleated" film from surf clams because it is unpleasant in the mouth. It is worth the effort. Be careful with remaining sand grains as well.

Spicy and sour dressing enchances the natural sweetness of surf clams.

SURF CLAM SALAD

● **Ingredients** ● 4 servings

8 fresh surf clams

DRESSING

    4 tablespoons mayonnaise

    1/2 teaspoon mustard

    Salt and peppar

GARNISH

    Red bell pepper

    3 lemon slices

    3 shiso (perrila) leaves

Ingredients ● ● 4 servings

400 grams(13oz) cabbage

100 grams(3 1/3 oz) bacon

2 green bell peppers

1 red bell pepper

1 tablespoon vegetable oil

1 tablespoon rice wine

1/2 cup chicken stock

1 tablespoon soy sauce

Pinch sugar, MSG, and pepper

This will surely become a favorite family dish you can cook in a jiffy.
Fry bacon well to bring out its aroma.

CABBAGE AND BACON

● Directions ●

CUT INGREDIENTS

❶ Wash cabbage leaves and drain well; tear into bite size pieces (A).

❷ Slice bacon thinly and cut into bite size pieces. Core and seed bell peppers and cut into wedges. Cut again diagonally into halves (B).

BLANCH CABBAGE

❸ Drop cabbage pieces in a wok of boiling water, blanch for 30 seconds, no longer; drain in a colander (C).

STIR-FRY

❹ Heat the wok until very hot. Add vegetable oil; turn off flame and stir-fry bacon.

❺ When the aroma of bacon is released, add cabbage and bell peppers; stir-fry over high heat.

❻ Season with rice wine, stock, soy sauce, sugar and MSG. Sprinkle generously with pepper.

Ⓐ

Ⓑ

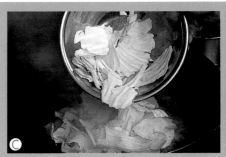

Ⓒ

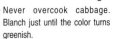

HELPFUL HINT

★ Never overcook cabbage. Blanch just until the color turns greenish.

Ingredients 4 servings

600 grams (1 1/3 pounds) pork sirloin
MARINADE
  1 teaspoon shaohsing wine
  2 teaspoons salt
  1/2 teaspoon soy sauce
  Dash sesame oil
  75 grams (2 1/2 ounces) sugar
  1/4 egg, beaten
  20 grams (2/3 ounce) miso (bean paste)
  Pinch five-spice powder
  Few drops red food coloring
CONDIMENTS
  Cucumber and green onion

The gourmets' favorite Char Shiu or Chinese barbecued roast pork can be cooked in your toaster-oven. Great for fried rice or noodles

SHU'S SPECIAL CHAR SHIU (BARBECUED PORK)

Directions

MARINATE MEAT

❶ Trim away fat and cut into three slices, each 2.5cm (1" inch) thick (A).

❷ In a large bowl combine ingredients for marinade and stir until smooth and slightly thickened (B).

❸ Add pork to the marinade sauce and let stand for 6 hours or overnight (C).

❹ Drain meat; turn over and drain completely (D).

GRILL MEAT

❺ Line the baking sheet with aluminum foil and roast meat for about 10 minutes (E).

❻ Turn over and roast a further 12-13 minutes. Check doneness by inserting a skewer: when the liquid runs clear, the meat is done (F).

PLACE ON A PLATE

❼ Slice the pork and place on a serving plate. Garnish with shredded cucumber and green onion.

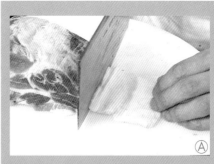

HELPFUL HINT

★ In summer, refrigerate the meat while marinating. In any season, do not marinate too long. If you keep it all day the marinade will become watery. This means the juice of the meat has been lost.

PROBLEMS TO AVOID

★ If the meat is not drained completely, it will scorch when grilled.

Ingredients   4 servings

2 medium tomatoes
50 grams (1 2/3 oz) softened cloud ears
3 eggs
1/3 teaspoon salt
1 teaspoon soy sauce

COOKING SAUCE
  1/3 cup chicken stock
  Pinch salt
  Pinch sugar and MSG
  1 tablespoon dissolved cornstarch
2 tablespoons vegetable oil
Fresh coriander

The tangy taste of tomato excites your appetite. Combine all seasonings before cooking for quick stir-frying. This will result in a soft and fluffy egg dish.

TOMATOES AND EGGS

 Directions

CUT INGREDIENTS

❶ Remove cores from tomatoes, cut into halves, then into 7-8mm(1/3") slices (A).

❷ Soak dried cloud ears in water until soft, and cut large ones into 2-3 pieces.

❸ In a small bowl, break eggs. Add salt and soy sauce; beat well. (B)

PREPARE COOKING SAUCE

❹ In another bowl, add stock, salt, sugar and MSG. Mix well and add dissolved cornstarch.

NOW STIR-FRY

❺ Heat wok until very hot and add vegetable oil. Pour in egg mixture. When the edges are set, add tomatoes and cloud ears (D).

❻ Stir in a long stroking motion until the eggs are half set; add cooking sauce (E).

❼ Stir quickly and transfer to a serving dish while the eggs are fluffy. Sprinkle with chopped coriander (F).

Ⓐ

Ⓑ

Ⓒ

CHEF'S SECRET

★ Dissolved cornstarch will make the eggs slide smoothly in your mouth.

Ingredients
4 servings

4 scallops
16 fresh shiso leaves
1 cup flour for tempura
Pinch salt
3/4 cup water
1 tablespoon vegetable oil
Oil for deep-frying
Boston lettuce
Lemon
Salt
DIPPING SAUCE
    Soy sauce
    Chili oil

The fresh fragrance of shiso gives lightness to deep-fried dishes. Perfect as an appetizer.

FRIED SCALLOPS IN SHISO LEAVES

Directions

PREPARE SCALLOPS

❶ Cut scallops lengthwise in half, then again into halves (A).

❷ Roll shiso around each scallop slice (B).

COAT WITH BATTER

❸ In a bowl mix flour for tempura, salt and water. Add vegetable oil and blend well.

❹ Dip each scallop slice in batter and coat thoroughly.

DEEP-FRY

❺ Heat oil to 170℃(340° F) and deep-fry scallops for about 3 minutes; drain well (E).

❻ Place on a serving dish accompanied with Boston lettuce leaves, lemon wedges, and salt. Serve with soy sauce and chili oil mixture.

Ⓐ Ⓑ Ⓒ

Ⓓ

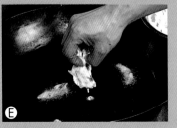

Ⓔ

CHEF'S SECRET

★ To make a fluffy and glossy tempura batter, combine 1 cup plain flour, 2 table-spoons corn starch 1 1/2 teaspoons baking powder and 2 tablespoons wheat starch.

CHEF'S SECRET

★ This recipe uses duck eggs preserved in lime, salt and other seasonings. If not available, make your own with chicken eggs: In a jar, dissolve salt in warm water to saturation and cool. Add eggs and put a weight on top. Soak eggs for about a month.

 Directions

"KNEAD" MINCED MEAT

❶ Crack eggs into a small bowl (A).

❷ In a large bowl add minced pork and half amount of egg white (B).

❸ Using your hand, mix well in a kneading motion (C).

STEAM MEAT

❹ On a chopping board press egg yolks with the side of a knife, gently sliding back and forth until each yolk is 7-8cm (2 1/2"-3") wide (D and E).

❺ In an oven-proof dish, spread meat mixture evenly and top with pressed egg yolks. Put in a boiling steamer and steam about 15 minutes.

❻ When cooked, speckle with coriander leaves.

Seasonings are reduced because of the salt content of the eggs.

STEAMED MEAT LOAF WITH PRESERVED DUCK EGGS

● **Ingredients** ● 4 servings

4 salt-preserved eggs
450 grams (1lb) minced pork
SEASONINGS
    1 teaspoon MSG
    Dash sesame oil
    Pinch sugar
    Pinch pepper
    3 tablespoons cornstarch
Fresh coriander

Ingredients

4 servings

400 grams (13 oz) chicken thigh, deboned

MARINADE

   Pinch salt, pepper, MSG

   1 teaspoon rice wine

   Dash sesame oil

   1 tablespoon cornstarch

   1 tablespoon vegetable oil

1/2 egg, beaten

Cornstarch for dusting

Oil for deep-frying

SAUCE

   1/2 tablespoon vegetable oil

   1 tablespoon orange curaçao

   1/2 cup chicken stock

   1/2 cup orange juice

   Pinch sugar

   2 teaspoons dissolved cornstarch

Orange, sliced

Candied cherries

Chicken and orange have a natural affinity. Do not "soak" in sauce too long and enjoy the crispness of chicken.

CHICKEN IN ORANGE SAUCE

Directions

CUT CHICKEN

❶ Cut into thickness and slice horizontally in half (A).

❷ Cut crisscross scores on a side of chicken and cut in half. Cut into 3cm (1 1/8") wide strips (B).

DUST WITH CORNSTARCH

❸ In a bowl, add all marinade ingredients and chicken pieces. Add beaten egg and mix well.

❹ Dust each piece with cornstarch and hold tightly in your hand to straighten the shape (C).

DEEP-FRY

❺ Heat oil to 180℃(350° F) and gently slide in coated chicken away from you (D).

❻ When the surface is set, lower the heat and cook well. Drain.

MAKE ORANGE SAUCE

❼ In a small pot, bring vegetable oil, orange curaçao and chicken stock to the boil. Add orange juice (E).

❽ Check the taste and add sugar accordingl . Thicken with dissolved cornstarch (F).

❾ On a serving dish, lay thinly sliced orange and top with chicken. Pour over the sauce and garnish with candied cherries.

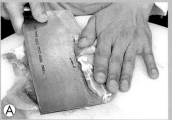
(A)

(B)

(C)

(D)

PROBLEMS TO AVOID

★ Dust with cornstarch just before frying, and hold firmly so the finished pieces will be straight.

HELPFUL HINT

★ Be sure to check the sweetness of the orange juice you use since it greatly depends on the brand. Add sugar if needed, but just enough to soften the sourness.

Ingredients

4 servings

400grams (13oz) beef, thinly sliced
1/2 red bell pepper
1 green bell pepper
2 dried shiitake mushrooms, soaked
    in water
1/4 stalk green onion
50 grams (1 1/3 oz) bamboo shoot
16 wonton skins
Oil for frying
MARINADE FOR BEEF
    Pinch each salt, sugar, MSG, and
      pepper
    1 tablespoon rice wine
    1 tablespoon soy sauce

1 teaspoon baking soda
1/2 cup water
Dash sesame oil
1/2 egg, beaten
1 tablespoon cornstarch
1 tablespoon vegetable oil
2 tablespoons vegetable oil
1/2 teaspoon each minced garlic and
    fresh ginger
1 tablespoon rice wine
1/2 tablespoon oyster sauce
1 cup beef or chicken stock
1 1/2 dissolved cornstarch

This is a popular Chinese dish with a
new twist. Add it to your repertoire.

SHREDDED BEEF ON CRISP SHELLS

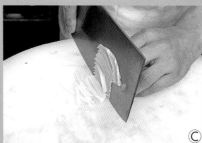

Directions

CUT UP INGREDIENTS

❶ Shred beef, bell peppers and softened shiitake
mushrooms. Cut green onion into 6-7cm(about 2 1/2")
lengths, split in half and shred; blanch in cold water (A).

❷ Slice bamboo shoot thinly, layer each slice sliding a
little, and shred (B and C).

DEEP-FRY WONTON SKINS

❸ Heat oil to 130-140℃(260-280° F) and deep-fry wonton
skins, one by one so they do not stick each other (D).

❹ Fry until crisp, then drain.

NOW STIR-FRY

❺ In a bowl, add marinade ingredients and mix well.

❻ Heat wok until very hot. Add vegetable oil and stir-fry
beef. Add minced garlic and ginger and continue
sautéeing (F).

❼ Add bell peppers, shiitake mushrooms and bamboo
shoots. Pour in rice wine, soy sauce, oyster sauce and
beef stock, and cook for 3-5 minutes. Drizzle in
dissolved cornstarch quickly stirring to thicken the sauce
evenly.

❽ Place in a serving dish accompanied with drained green
onion. Place one portion on a fried shell and eat.

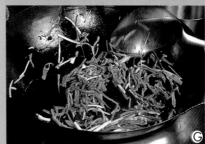

CHEF'S SECRET

★ When slicing bamboo
shoot thinly, hold it with
your fingers and at the
same time press the
chopping board with the
bottom of your palm.
This way it will stay in its
place.

HELPFUL HINT

★ Season a little heavier
than usual as deep-fried
wrappers will absorb the
sauce.

Ingredients

4 servings

3 stalks celery

1/2 stalk green onion

1/2 red bell pepper

1 green bell pepper

3 calamari

2 tablespoons vegetable oil

1 tablespoon rice wine

1 cup chicken stock

1/2 teaspoon salt

Pinch pepper, MSG

Few drops soy sauce

Cook briefly to enjoy the crispness of the celery and the tenderness of the calamari.

CELERY AND CALAMARI

Directions

CUT INGREDIENTS

❶ Lightly peel celery and slice diagonally. Split wider part in half, then slice (A and B).

❷ Slice green onion diagonally. Cut bell peppers into 4 or 6 wedges; then diagonally into halves.

❸ Holding calamari, pull out tentacles together with guts. Remove cartilage. Pull the triangle part down to peel the skin (C).

❹ Cut in half and score vertically. Holding the cleaver at a slant, cut into 1.5cm(5/8") widths (D).

PARBOIL

❺ In a wok, bring water to the boil. Add few drops of vegetable oil (not listed above) and cook celery less than a minute; drain. In the same pot, boil calamari for 1 - 2 minutes and drain (E).

STIR-FRY

❻ Heat wok well and add vegetable oil. Stir-fry calamari, then add celery (F).

❼ Season with rice wine, stock, salt, MSG and pepper. Drizzle in soy sauce from the sides of wok and briefly stir-fry (G).

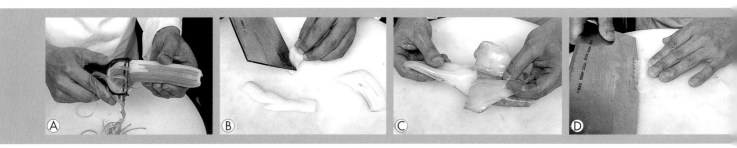

Ⓐ Ⓑ Ⓒ Ⓓ

CHEF'S SECRET

★Score calamari lightly all over before cutting to size. This will allow a clear pattern when cooked.

HELPFUL HINT

★ By drizzling soy sauce into the sides of the wok, a savory aroma will be released and enhance the flavor.

Ingredients ● 4 servings

400grams (13 oz) shrimp

1 teaspoon salt

Pinch MSG

2 tablespoons lard

1 tablespoon cornstarch

1 egg white

4 sheets grilled nori

2 tablespoons vegetable oil

Lettuce, lemon, and parsley

Crisp grilled nori and shrimp
release their savory aroma.

SHRIMP ROLLS

● Directions ●

MAKE SHRIMP PASTE

❶ Shell and devein shrimp. On a chopping
board, press down with a flat side of cleaver;
chop finely (A).

❷ Pound with the blunt edge of cleaver (B).

❸ In a bowl, knead shrimp until smooth, and add
salt, MSG, lard, cornstarch and egg white.

ROLL WITH NORI

❹ Lay a sheet of nori and spread shrimp paste in
a thin, even layer (C).

❺ Apply a dab of shrimp paste along far edge to
work as glue, and roll up away from you.
Secure the end (D).

❻ If wrapping from both sides, make a mound in
center and stick nori over on the shrimp paste
(E). Make 4 rolls.

COOK

❼ Heat wok well and add vegetable oil. Tilt the
wok so the oil spreads evenly. Reduce heat
and add rolls. Shake the wok to cook
thoroughly (F).

❽ Cut into bite-size slices and place on a serving
plate. Garnish with lettuce leaves, lemon and
parsley.

HELPFUL HINT

★ Too much paste on the edge of the
nori will be pushed out when rolled up.
Spread a thin coat of shrimp for a neat
roll.

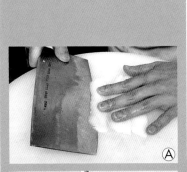

CHEF'S SECRET

★ By scoring the cuttlefish, each piece will have a decorative pattern when deep-fried.

 Directions

CUT UP CUTTLEFISH

❶ Cut crisscross scores over cuttlefish, then cut into 1cm (1/2"), holding the cleaver at a slant (A).

COAT THE CUTTLEFISH

❷ In a bowl place cuttlefish and add five-spice powder, salt, MSG, soy sauce, rice wine, sesame oil and egg (B).

DEEP-FRY

❸ Add cornstarch and mix well (C and D).

❹ Heat oil to 180℃(360° F) and deep-fry cuttlefish pieces until crisp; drain and serve.

F i v e - s p i c e powder

Moist and tender cuttlefish with an aroma from a special five-spice powder.

CUTTLEFISH DEEP-FRIED WITH FIVE-SPICE POWDER

 Ingredients 4 servings

200 grams(7 oz) cuttlefish

1/4 teaspoon five-spice powder

Pinch salt and MSG

1 teaspoon soy sauce

1 teaspoon rice wine

Dash sesame oil

1 egg, beaten

5 tablespoons cornstarch

Oil for frying

2 shiso(perrila) leaves

● Ingredients ●

4 servings

200grams(7 oz) shrimp

MARINADE FOR SHRIMP

   1/2 teaspoon baking soda

   Pinch each salt, MSG, pepper

   Dash sesame oil

   1/2 egg white

   1/2 tablespoon cornstarch

   1 tablespoon vegetable oil

1 tomato

10 snow peas

20 grams(2/3 oz) canned mushrooms, sliced

1/4 green onion

COOKING SAUCE

   1 cup chicken stock

   Dash soy sauce, salt, MSG, sugar

   1/2 tablespoon vinegar

   1 tablespoon vegetable oil

   1/2 teaspoon each minced garlic and ginger

1 teaspoon rice wine

The tartness of tomato enhances the flavor of shrimp.

SHRIMP AND TOMATO

● Directions ●

MARINATE SHRIMP

❶ In a bowl, add shrimp and baking soda, mix well and add remaining ingredients; set aside for about 20-30 minutes (A).

CUT INGREDIENTS

❷ Peel tomato: Insert chopsticks or a fork and dip into hot water; take out immediately. The skin now peels easily (B).

❸ Cut into wedges and then into halves (C).

❹ String snow peas and blanch in boiling water. Drain canned mushroom slices. Cut green onion diagonally into 1cm (3/8") slices.

PREPARE COOKING SAUCE

❺ Mix cooking sauce ingredients in a bowl (D).

STIR-FRY

❻ Heat wok well, pour vegetable oil and stir-fry snow peas, then mushrooms.

❼ Add minced garlic and ginger. When the aroma is released, add tomato and stir-fry.

❽ Pour over rice wine and cooking sauce, and stir-fry quickly (E).

Ⓐ

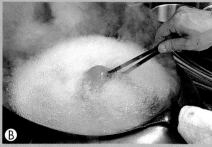
Ⓑ

Ⓒ

CHEF'S SECRET

★ Baking soda will give shrimp a springy texture.

Ingredients

4 servings

1 fresh crab (Dungeness)

10cm(4") green onion

1 small piece fresh ginger

1 red bell pepper

1 green bell pepper

Cornstarch for dusting

Oil for frying

1 tablespoon black beans

2 tablespoons rice wine

3/4 cup chicken stock

1 tablespoon soy sauce

1/2 tablespoon oyster sauce

1 heaped teaspoon sugar

1/2 teaspoon MSG

Pinch pepper

Dash soy sauce

If Dungeness crab is not available, use any fresh crab.

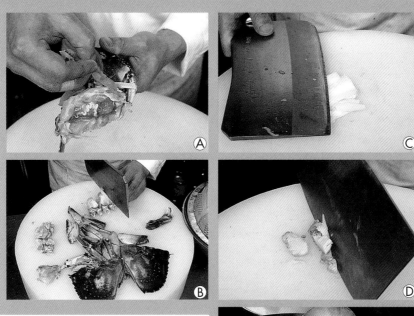

A mouth-watering spicy crab dish. Go ahead, eat with your fingers! The key is stir-frying the black beans well enough to extract the aroma.

STIR-FRIED CRAB WITH BLACK BEANS
● **Directions** ●

CUT INGREDIENTS

❶ Cut crab in half and remove top shell. Remove mouth and tapered gills surrounding the meat cells (A).

❷ Separate legs at joints. Cut them into appropriate lengths and then lengthwise into halves. Cut body meat into bite-size pieces (B).

❸ Using the side of a cleaver, press green onion and ginger, then chop coarsely (C and D).

❹ Seed bell peppers and cut into 2 cm(3/4 inch) squares.

DEEP-FRY CRAB

❺ Dust crab evenly with cornstarch. Deep-fry in 180℃(360°F) oil. (E)

❻ When the crab turns reddish, add chopped green onion and ginger. Deep-fry until the crab is cooked; drain (F).

STIR-FRY

❼ Pour the frying oil back into oil pot. Heat the wok again and stir-fry black beans. Add crab, green onion and ginger; then add bell peppers (G).

❽ Pour in rice wine and chicken stock. Bring to the boil and season with oyster sauce, sugar, MSG and pepper. Add soy sauce, checking the taste (H).

❾ Cover and cook until the sauce thickens. Place on a serving plate (I).

CHEF'S SECRET

★ By deep-frying green onion and ginger together with crab, the smell of crab will be softened and the oil itself can be used for other cooking with its light onion and ginger scent.

Ingredients

4 servings

2 cakes konnyaku

4 dried shiitake mushrooms, soaked in water

1/2 green onion

10 string beans

150 grams(5 oz) minced pork

SEASONINGS FOR PORK

    1/3 teaspoon salt

    Pinch each pepper and MSG

    Dash sesame oil

1 tablespoon vegetable oil

1 teaspoon hot bean sauce

COOKING SAUCE

    1 tablespoon rice wine

    1 1/2 cups chicken stock

    1/2 tablespoon soy sauce

    1 teaspoon oyster sauce

    Pinch each sugar, MSG and pepper

    Dash sesame oil

A hot, spicy, and chewy konnyaku dish for calorie watchers. This is a unique version of the well-known Mapo Tofu.

MAPO KONNYAKU

Directions

CUT INGREDIENTS

❶ Cut each konnyaku cake into 4 lengthwise. Cut at a slant to make diamonds (A).

❷ Cut softened shiitake mushrooms into 1.5cm (3/4") squares, green onion into 1cm (1/2") lengths. Cook string beans in boiling water and cut into 1cm (1/2") lengths.

STIR-FRY MEAT AND KONNYAKU

❸ In a bowl combine minced pork and seasonings.

❹ Heat wok until very hot, add vegetable oil and stir-fry minced meat until it crumbles (B).

❺ Add minced garlic and hot bean sauce. When the aroma is released, add konnyaku, shiitake mushrooms, and long onion and stir-fry (C).

ADD SEASONINGS

❻ Add cooking sauce ingredients and cook until the sauce is absorbed. Sprinkle in pepper.

❼ Finally add string beans and sprinkle with sesame oil (D).

Ⓐ

Ⓑ

Ⓒ

HELPFUL HINT

★ It is important to stir-fry konnyaku very well so it will hold the seasonings.

PROBLEMS TO AVOID

★ Season on the heavy side as konnyaku has a bland taste.

Ingredients  4 servings

400 grams (13 oz) beef filet
Pinch salt, and pepper
Dash rice wine
1/2 tablespoon soy sauce
1 teaspoon Chinese soy sauce
2 tablespoons vegetable oil
1 spring roll skins
Oil for deep-frying
Red and green bell peppers, sliced
Cucumbers, shredded
Red onion, sliced
Green onion
Candied cherries

Bite-size Chinese steak with original, richly flavored sauce.

FILLET STEAK

Directions

COOK BEEF

❶ Sprinkle beef with salt and pepper. In a small bowl, combine rice wine, soy sauce and Chinese soy sauce and marinate for 10 minute (A).

❷ Heat wok until very hot and add vegetable oil. Cook beef until the color just changes on the surface (B).

❸ Cut beef into 1cm (1/2") wide strips (C).

PREPARE CONDIMENTS

❹ Line a 12-13cm (about 5") diam. wire strainer with spring roll skin. Place a smaller metal strainer on top.

❺ Heat oil to 150℃(300°F) and deep-fry the skin holding the strainers together.

❻ Shred cucumber and slice red onion. Make a flower of green onion (use white part) by cutting slits lengthwise leaving 2cm (1") at the top.

❼ Place drained skins on serving plates. Fill each skin with beef strips. Garnish with shredded vegetables.

❽ Serve with sa cha sauce, pepper sauce or Japanese sauce (See page 38 for sauce recipes).

 Ⓐ

 Ⓑ

 Ⓒ

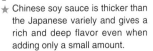

CHEF'S SECRET

★ Chinese soy sauce is thicker than the Japanese variely and gives a rich and deep flavor even when adding only a small amount.

HELPFUL HINT

★ Unlike other Chinese recipes, the steak is not cut up before cooking in this recipe. The beef should be cooked evenly before being cut into strips.

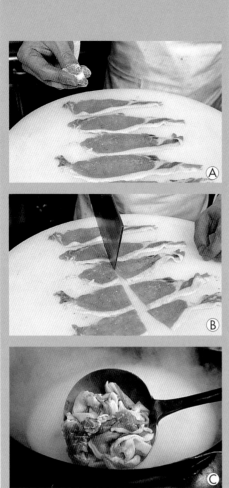

(A)

(B)

(C)

BOIL MEAT

❶ Sprinkle pork slices with salt and pepper, and set aside for 5-10 minutes (A).

❷ Cut each into halves or appropriate size (B).

❸ In a wok, bring water to the boil, cook pork slices separating them from each other. Skim foam and drain in a metal strainer (C).

PREPARE CONDIMENTS

❹ Shred daikon radish, cucumber and carrot, then mix together. Cut tomatoes into wedges.

❺ Place the meat and vegetables on a serving plate. Garnish with parsley and serve with chili sauce, sesame sauce and herbal sauce. Refer to page 39 for sauce recipes.

HELPFUL HINT

★ Serve piping hot, or for a summer dish the pork can be chilled thoroughly in the fridge and served as cold pork with cold dips.

This is a Chinese version of Shabu-Shabu, a popular Japanese hot pot dish. Enjoy a variety of dipping sauces. Serve hot or cold.

BOILED PORK SLICES

 **Ingredients** 4 servings

300grams (10 oz) pork loin, thinly sliced

Salt and pepper

Daikon radish

Cucumber

Carrot

Tomato

Parsley sprigs

Pour over steaks, salads or use as a dip for fried foods

My favorite Sauces

A sauce can turn a regular salad or steak into a special course. Make several sauces and enjoy the contrast of flavors, or prepare double portions and keep in the fridge for another day.

The following ingredients make three different sauces. Recommended for fillet steak on page 36.

P epper Sauce

Spicy black pepper excites your appetite.

● Ingredients ● 4 servings

1 teaspoon black pepper
1 tablespoon soy sauce
1/2 tablespoon oyster sauce
Pinch MSG
1/2 cup chicken stock

● Directions ●

❶ In a bowl, combine all ingredients except the stock.

❷ Stir in the stock and blend well.

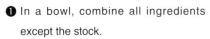

This pungent sauce allows the flavor of food to dominate.

S a Cha Sauce

● Ingredients ● 4 servings

1/2 teaspoon minced belgian shallot
1 teaspoon sa cha sauce (Chinese barbecue sauce)
1/2 cup chicken stock

● Directions ●

❶ In a bowl, combine all ingredients except the stock.

❷ Stir in the stock and blend well.

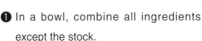

J apanese Sauce

For the day you feel like a lighter serve

● Ingredients ● 4 servings

1/2 tablespoon sesame oil
1 tablespoon soy sauce
Pinch pepper
1 tablespoon rice wine
1 teaspoon rice vinegar
1 teaspoon sugar
1/2 cup chicken stock

● Directions ●

❶ In a bowl, combine all ingredients except the stock.

❷ Stir in the stock and blend well.

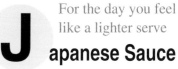
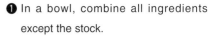

Three Sauces for Boiled Pork Slices (page 37) and Others

Adjust chili bean paste and sesame oil to taste

Hot Chili Sauce

🔴 **Ingredients** 🔴 4 servings

1/2 tablespoon hot bean paste
1 tablespoon rice wine
1 1/2 tablespoon soy sauce
Dash sesame oil
3/4 cup chicken stock
Green onion, sliced

🔴 **Directions** 🔴

❶ In a bowl, combine hot bean paste, rice wine and soy sauce. Stir in chicken stock.

❶ Blend until smooth.

Sweet and savory

Sesame Sauce

🔴 **Ingredients** 🔴 4 servings

3 tablespoons sesame paste
1 tablespoon sugar
1/2 tablespoon soy sauce
Pinch MSG
1/2 tablespoon rice vinegar
3/4 cup chicken stock

🔴 **Directions** 🔴

❶ In a bowl, combine sesame paste, sugar, soy sauce and MSG .

❷ Stir in rice vinegar.

❸ Add chicken stock in a thin stream and blend well until whitish in color. If the stock is added too fast the sauce will curdle.

You're sure to succeed!!

Add the ethnic flavor of coriander

Coriander Sauce

🔴 **Ingredients** 🔴 4 servings

2 tablespoons soy sauce
1 tablespoon sesame oil
3/4 cup chicken stock
1 tablespoon rice vinegar
Fresh coriander

🔴 **Directions** 🔴

❶ In a bowl combine soy sauce, sesame oil, and chicken stock. Add rice vinegar.

❷ Sprinkle with coriander leaves.

Ingredients
4 servings

300 grams(10 oz) beef uterus
Cornstarch
Rice vinegar
SEASONINGS FOR BEEF UTERUS
    1/2 teaspoon salt
    1 tablespoon rice wine
    1 teaspoon sesame oil
1 tablespoon sesame oil
1 teaspoon minced garlic
1 tablespoon black beans
1 tablespoon chili bean paste
COOKING SAUCE
    1 tablespoon rice wine
    1 cup chicken stock
    2 tablespoons soy sauce
    1 teaspoon oyster sauce
    Pinch MSG
1 tablespoon dissolved cornstarch
Cabbage, shredded
Parsley

Crunchy offal with the deep flavor of fermented black beans makes a good accompaniment for wines.

OFFAL IN BLACK BEAN SAUCE

Directions

CUT OFFAL

❶ Cut offal into bite size pieces, making incisions in the rounds (A).

❷ Coat with cornstarch. Wash offal in a bowl filled with rice vinegar. Rinse under running water and drain.

❸ In a bowl add offals and seasonings. Rub seasonings in and set aside (B).

❹ Cook in boiling water for 3-4 minutes and drain (C).

NOW STIR-FRY

❺ Heat wok until very hot and add 1 tablespoon sesame oil. Stir-fry minced garlic, black beans and hot bean paste (D).

❻ When the aroma is released add offal and stir-fry until well-done. Stir in cooking sauce ingredients and thicken the sauce with dissolved cornstarch (E).

❼ Place on a serving dish and garnish with cabbage and parsley.

CHEF'S SECRET

★ Season uterus before boiling to give flavor.

Ⓐ

Ⓑ

Ⓒ

Ⓓ

Ⓔ

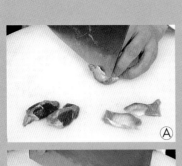

(A)

(B)

(C)

(D)

(E)

CHEF'S SECRET

★ A dash of rice wine added to the boiling water will remove the gizzard smell.

 Directions

CUT INGREDIENTS

❶ Trim away white, hard part of gizzards, and cut criss-cross scores on each surface (A and B).

❷ Cook in boiling water with a dash of rice wine. Drain when the surfaces turn whitish.

❸ Cut onion and bell peppers into 1.5-2cm (about 3/4") squares.

❹ Heat wok until very hot and add vegetable oil.

STIR-FRY

Stir-fry sliced cayenne peppers and gizzards (C).

❺ Sprinkle with soy sauce and stir in ginger (D and E).

❻ Stir in onion and bell peppers, then add cooking sauce ingredients. Thicken the sauce with dissolved cornstarch.

HELPFUL HINT

★ Since gizzards do not absorb flavors easily, stir-fry with soy sauce before adding other seasonings. This way the flavors will hold.

Hot and spicy gizzards.
Properly prepared gizzards are
pleasantly bouncy in your mouth.

MUSTARD GIZZARDS

 **Ingredients** 4 servings

300 grams(10 oz) gizzards
Dash rice wine
1/2 onion
1/2 red bell pepper
1 green bell pepper
1 tablespoon vegetable oil
1 teaspoon sliced cayenne pepper
Dash soy sauce
1 teaspoon minced fresh ginger
COOKING SAUCE
    1 teaspoon sugar
    1/2 teaspoon oyster sauce
    1 tablespoon soy sauce
    1/2 cup chicken stock
    1/2 teaspoon MSG
    Pinch pepper
3/4 tablespoon dissolved cornstarch

Ingredients

4 servings

1 cake firm tofu

2 dried shiitake mushrooms, softened

30 grams (1 oz) canned oyster
mushrooms

30 grams (1 oz) canned button
mushrooms

30 grams (1 oz) canned straw
mushrooms

2 sprigs komatsuna (Brassica
campetris) greens

10 grams (1/3 oz) carrot

1/4 stalk green onion

2 tablespoons vegetable oil

1/2 teaspoon each minced garlic and
ginger

COOKING SAUCE

1 tablespoon rice wine

1/2 cup chicken stock

1 tablespoon oyster sauce

Pinch each sugar, MSG and
pepper

1 1/2 tablespoons dissolved
cornstarch

Make a healthy dish using mushrooms
abundant in dietary fiber.
The key is in seasoning the tofu well.

BRAISED MUSHROOMS AND TOFU

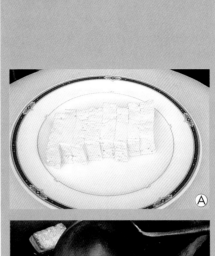

Directions

CUT INGREDIENTS

❶ Cut tofu into 1cm(3/8") wide strips and set aside to drain (A).

❷ Cut softened shiitake mushrooms into 4 or 6 wedges. Drain canned mushrooms.

❸ Cut *komatsuna* into 5-6cm (about 2") lengths. Cut carrot into thin rectangles, and green onion into diagonal slices.

STIR-FRY

❹ Heat wok until very hot and add vegetable oil. Slide in well-drained tofu and cook over high heat. When browned, reduce heat to medium and brown both sides (B).

❺ Stir in minced garlic and ginger. When the aroma is released, add mushrooms and vegetables and stir-fry.

❻ Add cooking sauce ingredients and cook for about 3 minutes until the tofu absorbs the flavor (C and D).

❼ Stir in dissolved cornstarch to thicken the sauce (E).

HELPFUL HINT

★ No weight is necessary to drain tofu. Just leave it in a dish or colander until excess moisture comes out.

PROBLEMS TO AVOID

★ Do not drop tofu in the center of wok as it will cause the hot oil to splatter. Gently slide in from the sides of wok.

Ingredients

4 servings

2 bok choy green

4 shiitake mushrooms

100grams(3 1/3 oz) shimeji mushrooms

5 snow peas

Carrot

1/4 stalk green onion

200 grams (7 oz) white meat fish

SEASONINGS FOR FISH

    Pinch each salt, MSG, and pepper

    1 teaspoon rice wine

    Dash sesame oil

    1/2 egg white

    1/2 teaspoon baking soda

1 tablespoon vegetable oil

Cornstarch

Vegetable oil

Pinch salt

MSG, pepper

1 tablespoon soy sauce

SAUCE

    1 tablespoon vegetable oil

    1 tablespoon rice wine

    1 cup chicken stock

    Salt and pepper

1 tablespoon dissolved cornstarch

WHITE FISH AND VEGETABLES

Directions

CUT INGREDIENTS

❶ Cut bok choy lengthwise into 4 or 6. Cut shiitake mushrooms into halves. Trim away root of shimeji mushrooms and tear into small pieces. String snow peas. Cut carrot into strips, green onion into diagonal slices.

❷ Cut fish into bite-size pieces and coat with seasoning ingredients. Dust with cornstarch (B).

PREPARE

❸ Heat wok until very hot, add vegetable oil and stir-fry mushrooms. Remove from wok when soft (C).

❹ In the wok add hot water and bring to the boil. Sprinkle salt and boil bok choy; remove and drain (D).

❺ In the same wok, boil snow peas, carrot, green onion and mushrooms, then remove and drain. Boil white meat fish in the same water (E and F).

STIR-FRY

❻ Heat the wok until very hot and add vegetable oil. Stir-fry green onion and boiled vegetables, excluding bok choy. Season with salt, MSG, pepper and soy sauce.

❼ Line a serving plate with drained bok choy and arrange vegetables. Top with white meat fish.

MAKE SAUCE

❽ Add vegetable oil in heated wok and stir in rice wine, beef stock, salt and MSG. Thicken with dissolved cornstarch.

❾ Pour over fish and vegetables (G).

CHEF'S SECRET

★ Cornstarch dusting of the fish works as a coating film and gives a springy texture.

 E
 F
 G

Ingredients — 4 servings

400 grams (13 oz) beef rib
2 potatoes
8 string beans
1/8 head Chinese cabbage
Beef stock
Vegetable oil
COOKING SAUCE
    3 cups beef stock
    1 tablespoon rice wine
    3 tablespoons soy sauce
    2 tablespoons oyster sauce
    1 tablespoon sugar

A home-cooked family favorite. Cook slowly so the flavor is fully absorbed in the fork-tender meat and potatoes. Oyster sauce adds richness.

POTATOES AND BEEF RIB

Directions

CUT INGREDIENTS

❶ Trim away extra fat from beef rib, and cut into large cubes (A).

❷ Peel potatoes and cut into slightly larger pieces than beef (B).

❸ Cook string beans in boiling water and cut into 3-4cm (1 1/4"-1 1/2") lengths. Cut Chinese cabbage into 3cm (1/4") wide strips and cook in boiling beef stock.

STIR-FRY

❹ Heat wok until very hot and add vegetable oil. Stir-fry beef over high heat until browned. Pour in hot water and boil for about 5 minutes; drain (C).

❺ In the heated wok, add salad oil and stir-fry potatoes until browned (D).

SIMMER

❻ In a saucepan add beef and cooking sauce; simmer for 1-2 hours.

❼ When the beef is tender add potatoes and cook a further 15-20 minutes until the potatoes are soft. Add string beans just before removing from the heat (E).

❾ Arrange Chinese cabbage in circle on a serving dish, place beef and potatoes in the center.

HELPFUL HINT

★ Stir-fry beef until the surface is just browned, then immediately pour in water. This boiling process removes fat and scum, resulting in a light and delicate taste.

46

CHEF'S SECRET

★ Remove the skin of beef liver before cooking. A tough texture will result if cooked with the skin on. If using pork liver, peeling is not necessary.

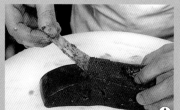

● Directions ●

CUT INGREDIENTS

❶ Skin beef liver and slice thinly (A).

❷ In a bowl combine liver, ginger juice and rice wine. Rub liver with your fingers, then wash in water and drain (B).

❸ Coat liver with cornstarch and cook in boiling water, until almost done; drain (C).

❹ Halve the length of pumpkin and then slice into 7-8mm (1/3") thicknesses. Heat oil and deep-fry until browned (D).

STIR-FRY

❺ Heat wok until very hot and add vegetable oil and hot bean paste. Stir-fry liver until well done (E).

❻ Add pumpkin and keep stirring. Stir in rice wine and cooking sauce (F).

❼ Keep stirring until the flavor is absorbed, then thicken the sauce with dissolved cornstarch.

An unusual combination of beef liver and pumpkin flavored with chili. The sweetness of the pumpkin softens the strong taste the liver.

BEEF LIVER AND PUMPKIN

● Ingredients ● 4 servings

200 grams(7 oz) beef liver
Dash each fresh ginger juice and rice wine
Cornstarch
200 grams (7 oz)pumpkin
Oil for frying
2 tablespoons vegetable oil
1 teaspoon hot bean paste
1 tablespoon rice wine
COOKING SAUCE (Blend ahead of cooking)
    1/2 cup beef stock
    1 tablespoon soy sauce
    Pinch each sugar and pepper
1/2 tablespoon dissolved cornstarch

47

Ingredients

4 servings

400 grams(13 oz) beef spareribs cut into pieces

MARINADE
　1/2 teaspoon salt
　Pinch each sugar and MSG
　1/2 teaspoon baking soda
　1/2 teaspoon soy sauce
　2 tablespoons water
　1/2 egg, beaten
　1 teaspoon vegetable oil

1 pack (100 grams, 3 1/3oz) maitake mushrooms
8 string beans
Vegetable oil
COOKING SAUCE
　2 tablespoons XO sauce
　1 teaspoon rice wine
　1/2 cup beef stock
　1/2 tablespoon oyster sauce
Pinch pepper

XO sauce makes this sparerib dish rich and flavorful, blending well with aromatic maitake mushrooms.

SPARERIBS IN XO SAUCE

Directions

MARINATE MEAT

❶ In a small bowl combine salt, sugar, MSG, soy sauce and water (A).

❷ In a larger bowl put spareribs and pour in marinade. Rub marinade into meat, then stir in beaten egg and vegetable oil; set aside while preparing vegetables (B).

PREPARE OTHER INGREDIENTS

❸ Cut maitake mushrooms into large pieces. Cook string beans in boiling water and cut into 4-5cm (about 2") length (C).

STIR-FRY

❹ Heat wok until very hot and add Vegetable oil. Stir-fry mushrooms until slightly soft. Pour in hot water and cook briefly; drain in a colander (D).

❺ In heated wok add vegetable oil and fry spareribs (E).

❻ When the meat is cooked, stir in XO sauce, stir-fry mushrooms and string beans together (F and G).

❼ Add remaining seasonings and stir-fry. Sprinkle with pepper to finish.

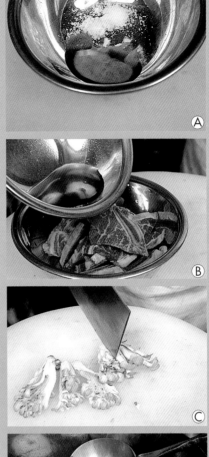

CHEF'S SECRET

★ Water and baking soda in the marinade make the meat tender and tasty.

HELPFUL HINT

★ *Maitake* mushrooms become crispy when fried but also absorb oil. It is advisable to remove oil by blanching in boiling water.

Ingredients 4 servings

150 grams (5 oz) fresh chestnuts

Oil for frying

3 dried shiitake mushrooms, softened

1/4 carrot

2 bok choy green

250 grams (8 oz) chicken

2 tablespoons vegetable oil

1 tablespoon rice wine

1 cups chicken stock

1 1/2 tablespoons soy sauce

Dissolved cornstarch

Dash sesame oil

You'll love even the sauce itself of this delicious braised dish, featuring the sweetness of chestnuts and a light and dry texture.

CHICKEN WITH CHESTNUTS

 Directions

DEEP-FRY CHESTNUTS

❶ Peel chestnuts and soak in water for about 1 hour to remove bitterness; wipe dry.

❷ Heat oil (use less than usual) to 160-170℃(325-340°F) and shallow-fry chestnuts until slightly browned (A).

CUT UP INGREDIENTS

❸ Cut shiitake mushrooms into halves or quarters. Cut carrot into rolling wedges and cook in boiling water. Divide bok choy into stalks and leaves, and cut each stalk lengthwise into 4 to 6.

❹ Cut chicken to match the size of chestnuts. Coat with a little soy sauce (not included above) (B).

STIR-FRY

❺ Heat wok until very hot and add vegetable oil. Stir-fry chicken until lightly browned.

❻ Add rice wine, chicken stock and soy sauce and simmer over low heat for about 10 minutes.

❼ Add chestnuts, mushrooms, carrot and bok choy. Check and adjust the taste (C).

❽ Thicken the sauce with dissolved cornstarch and sprinkle with sesame oil to finish (D).

PROBLEMS TO AVOID

★ Carefully fry chestnuts since they scorch easily due to high sugar content.

HELPFUL HINT

★ By frying chestnuts, the sweet flavor will be sealed in. Adjust the thickness of cornstarch according to the cooking sauce consistency.

Ingredients ● 4 servings

1 whole channal rockfish (about 200 grams,
   7 oz of any white meat fish)
Cornstarch
Vegetable oil
1 tablespoon rice wine
1 1/2 cups chicken stock
1 tablespoon soy sauce
1/2 green onion, cut into 5cm (2") lengths
COOKING SAUCE
   Pinch each sugar and MSG
   1 tablespoon oyster sauce
   1 teaspoon soy sauce
   1 teaspoon Chinese soy sauce
   Pinch pepper

Fish liver flavors this rich braised fish.

BRAISED ROCKFISH

● Directions ●

PREPARE FISH

❶ Cut an incision on one side of fish and remove scales and intestines. Set liver aside.

❷ Cut scores at a slant on both sides of fish so the seasonings will be absorbed (A).

❸ Using the side of a cleaver, crush liver, then chop (B).

❹ Dust the fish with cornstarch (C).

FRY FISH

❺ Heat wok until very hot and add vegetable oil. Fry fish, serving side first. When the surface becomes crisp and dry, turn over and cook the other side (D).

BRAISE WITH LIVER

❻ In a shallow pan place fish and add liver, rice wine, chicken stock, soy sauce and green onion. Cover and cook over low heat for 10 minutes.

❼ Add cooking sauce ingredients adjusting to taste (F).

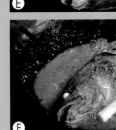

CHEF'S SECRET

★ Use liver as a seasoning. It creates a deep flavor.

HELPFUL HINT

★ When frying the fish, place it incised side up so the liquid does not flow. This way the fish will not scorch on the pan and results in a crisp surface.

★ Soy sauce sprinkled over tofu accelerates the draining as well as marinating.

CHEF'S SECRET

★ Granulated chicken stock added to batter enhances the flavor of tofu. Vegetable oil is also added to make a smooth coating.

● Directions ●

SEASON TOFU

❶ Cut tofu lengthwise in half, then into 2cm (1") cubes.

❷ In a small bowl, place tofu and sprinkle with soy sauce; set aside until water drains out (A).

COAT WITH BATTER

❸ In a bowl, combine tempura flour, granulated chicken stock, water and vegetable oil (B).

❹ Add tofu and coat with batter (C).

DEEP-FRY TOFU

❺ Heat oil to 180℃ (350°F) and deep-fry tofu (D).

❻ Drop remaining batter into oil to make a thick coating, and deep-fry until crisp (E).

❼ In a serving dish, place *tofu*. Garnish with lettuce leaves and parsley. Serve with the dip (combine dipping sauce ingredients).

Tempura of *tofu*, with a crunchy coating. Serve steaming hot with Chinese dip.

TOFU TEMPURA

● Ingredients ● 4 servings

1 cake firm tofu
2 tablespoons soy sauce
BATTER
    1 cup tempura flour
    1 teaspoon granulated chicken stock
    3/4 cup water
    1 tablespoon vegetable oil
Oil for frying
Lettuce and parsley
DIPPING SAUCE
    2 tablespoons rice vinegar
    1 tablespoon soy sauce
    Pinch sugar
    Minced green onion

Ingredients

4 servings

4 bunches garlic chives
Pinch salt and MSG
1 teaspoon rice wine
1 teaspoon soy sauce

Dash sesame oil
2 eggs
Flour dissolved in water
Tomato
Vegetable oil

Garlic chives are a warehouse of vitamins. The strong flavor is softened with sesame oil and eggs.

EGG ROLLS WITH GARLIC CHIVES

Directions

SEASON GARLIC CHIVES

❶ In boiling water cook chives root ends first. When the ends become soft, allow the rest to cook briefly until soft (A).

❷ Drain and squeeze out water. Cut into 2-3cm (about 2") lengths and put in a bowl. Add salt, MSG, rice wine, soy sauce and sesame oil and mix well (B).

ROLL WITH THIN OMELET

❸ Heat wok until very hot and add a little vegetable oil. Pour beaten eggs, a quarter amount at a time and make 4 thin omelets (C).

❹ When the omelets are cooled, lay one sheet on a chopping board. Place a quarter amount of garlic chives on omelet and roll away from you. Use dissolved flour as a glue on the edge of omelet (D and E).

FRY EGG ROLLS

❺ In a heated pan add vegetable oil and fry the egg rolls. When browned, turn over and fry the other side (F).

❻ Cut rolls into 3cm (about 1") lengths and place on a serving plate. Garnish with tomato wedges.

Ⓐ

Ⓑ

Ⓒ

HELPFUL HINT
★ Season garlic chives well since the eggs are not seasoned.

Ingredients ● 4 servings

4 dried scallops
Chicken stock
1/2 daikon radish
Pinch salt
1 radish
Bean sprouts, carrot, snow peas
Fresh coriander

Dried scallops are the surprise ingredient that gives a delicate flavor to other ingredients.

STEAMED DAIKON WITH SCALLOPS

● Directions ●

SOFTEN SCALLOPS

❶ In a bowl pour hot chicken stock and soak dried scallops; let stand until soft (A).

SCOOP OUT DAIKON

❷ Slice daikon into 2-3cm(1") widths. In the center of each round, press down a bottle cap and mark circles (B).

❸ Using a paring cleaver, cut along the circle towards the other side. Press the bottle cap from the other side to cut out (C).

❹ Bring water to the boil and add a pinch of salt. Boil daikon until almost done (D).

COOK DAIKON

❺ Remove daikon and stuff with scallop. Place stuffed daikon on a heat-proof container, and pour over scallop soaking water (E and F).

❻ Steam in a steamer, for about 15 minutes (G).

❼ Reheat the liquid in the heat-proof container and season with salt.

PREPARE GARNISH

❽ Make decorative crisscross scores on radish. Boil bean sprouts, carrot and snow peas.

❾ On a serving plate place steamed daikon and sprinkle with fresh coriander leaves. Garnish with vegetables and pour over the juice.

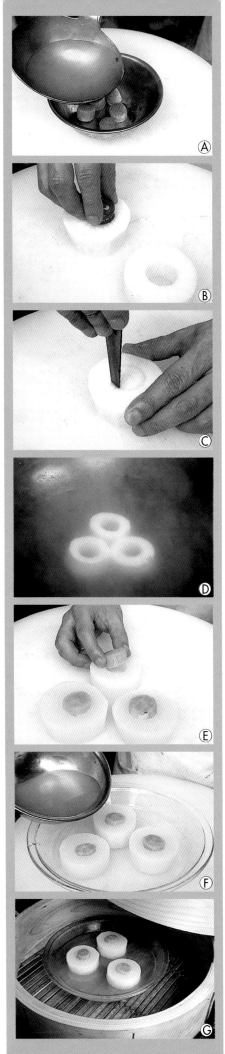

(A)
(B)
(C)
(D)
(E)
(F)
(G)

CHEF'S SECRET

★ If using small scallops, do not cut through daikon but down to a half depth by inserting a knife horizontally half-way down and press down a bottle cap.

● Ingredients ● 4 servings

200 grams(7 oz) beef shank
SPECIAL SAUCE
    180cc (6 oz) shaohsing wine
    250cc(8 oz) soy sauce
    125 grams(4 oz) crystal brown sugar
    1 teaspoon five-spice powder
    200cc (7 oz) water
1 tomato
Cucumber and lettuce
Lemon wedges

Shu-san's special sauce tastes so mild and deep that you will want to save a lot in the fridge for later use.

BEEF SHANK STEAMED IN SPECIAL SAUCE

● Directions ●

PARBOIL SHANK

❶ Trim away extra fat from shank, and cut into long strips parallel to the grain (A).

❷ In a large amount of boiling water cook shank 7-8 minutes, skimming foam constantly, until the surface turns whitish and the meat shrinks; drain (B and C).

SIMMER IN SPECIAL SAUCE

❸ In the a saucepan place sauce ingredients and meat, simmer for 2 hours; remove from heat and allow to cool soaked in sauce (E).

❹ Drain meat and slice thinly (F).

❺ Place on a serving plate and garnish with lettuce, half-moon cut tomato, sliced cucumber and lemon wedges.

HELPFUL HINT

★ Wide strips of meat will curl when cooked. Cut as narrow as possible so they remain straight.

PROBLEMS TO AVOID

★ At this stage do not cook completely, or the flavor will seep out into the water.

HELPFUL HINT

★ Marinate meat or fish before stir-frying for a deeper flavor. If using salted fish, marinating is not necessary.

(A)

(B)

(C)

(D)

(E)

PROBLEMS TO AVOID

★ Be sure to check the taste of cooking sauce before adding to wok. It is difficult to adjust the taste after the sauce is thickened.

 Directions

CUT INGREDIENTS

❶ Cut each cod fillet into 4-5 bite-size pieces. Combine marinade ingredients and add cod pieces. Set aside (A).

❷ Divide bok choy into stalks and leaves. Cut stalks lengthwise into 4-6 pieces. Cut carrot into rectangles, green onion into diagonal slices.

MAKE COOKING SAUCE

❸ In a small bowl, combine all sauce ingredients (B).

PARBOIL GREENS

❹ Heat wok until very hot and briefly stir-fry bok choy; pour in hot water and salt and cook; remove and drain (C).

❺ In the same water cook cod; remove and drain (D).

STIR-FRY

❻ Heat wok until very hot, add vegetable oil and stir-fry carrot, green onion, ginger, and bok choy in order.

❼ Add cod and keep stir-frying. Pour in cooking sauce and cook until the flavor is absorbed (E).

● **Ingredients** ● 4 servings

4 fillets cod
MARINADE
    Pinch each salt, MSG, and pepper
    1 teaspoon rice wine
    Dash sesame oil
    1/2 egg white
    1 teaspoon baking soda
    1/2 tablespoon cornstarch
    1 tablespoon vegetable oil
4 bok choy green
Carrot
1/4 green onion
Small piece of ginger, sliced
COOKING SAUCE
    1/2 cup chicken stock
    1/2 teaspoon salt
    Pinch each pepper and MSG
    1 teaspoon oyster sauce
    1 teaspoon soy sauce
Vegetable oil
Pinch salt

The plain taste of cod can be very appealing when stir-fried in a flavorful cooking sauce. A quick and easy dish.

COD WITH BOK CHOY

● Ingredients ●

4 servings

200 grams(7 oz) pork, thinly sliced
MARINADE
   Pinch each salt, MSG and pepper
   1 teaspoon rice wine
   1 teaspoon soy sauce
   Dash sesame oil
   1/2 egg, lightly beaten
   1 teaspoon cornstarch
   1 tablespoon vegetable oil
1 bunch chrysanthemum leaves
1/4 carrot
1/4 green onion

1 tablespoon vegetable oil
1/2 teaspoon each minced garlic and
   ginger
SEASONINGS
   1 tablespoon soy sauce
   1/2 tablespoon oyster sauce
   Pinch each pepper, sugar and MSG
   1/2 cup chicken stock
1 tablespoon dissolved cornstarch
Dash sesame oil

Strongly scented ingredients such as chrysanthemum leaves, green onion and pork can create a delightful aroma when combined in harmony.

PORK AND CHRYSANTHEMUM LEAVES

● Directions ●

CUT INGREDIENTS

❶ Cut pork into bite size pieces and add to a bowl. Stir in marinade ingredients and set aside (A).

❷ Discard hard ends of chrysanthemum leaves and cut into 3 or 4 lengthwise. Blanch in boiling water (B).

❸ Cut carrot into rectangles and green onion into diagonal slices.

STIR-FRY

❹ Heat wok until very hot and add vegetable oil.

Stir-fry pork until well done (C).

❺ Add carrot and green onion and continue cooking. When the onion becomes soft, stir in minced garlic and ginger and extract the aroma (D and E).

SEASON TO TASTE

❻ Add chrysanthemum leaves, then stir in seasonings. Thicken the sauce with dissolved cornstarch and sprinkle with sesame oil to finish (F).

Ⓐ

Ⓑ

Ⓒ

HELPFUL HINT

★ Marinating pork in soy sauce will give a pleasant aroma when cooked.

PROBLEMS TO AVOID

★ Cook green onion at this stage, or it will not soften enough.

● **Ingredients** ● 4-5 servings

1 whole chicken, giblets removed

Pinch each salt and MSG

2 tablespoons rice wine

Dash sesame oil

1/2 stalk green onion

Knob of ginger

SAUCE

    Few drops red food coloring

    2 tablespoons corn syrup

    3 cups hot water

    1 tablespoon rice vinegar

Great roast chicken Chinese style. Marinating with green onion and ginger is the key to success.

ROAST CHICKEN

Directions

PREPARE CHICKEN

❶ Put chicken in a bowl and rub with salt, MSG, rice wine and sesame oil.

❷ Using the side of a cleaver, crush green onion and ginger, then mince. Rub into chicken (A).

❸ Place green onion and ginger inside the chicken and rub together with the juices; let stand overnight (B).

❹ Remove green onion and ginger and wash chicken; drain (C).

PARBOIL AND SEASON

❺ Insert metal hooks under chicken wings and place in ample boiling water. Pour hot water over the top part floating above water. Keep pouring for about 3 minutes until the skin is cooked (D and E).

❻ Drain chicken. Combine sauce ingredients. Holding the metal hooks, coat the chicken evenly with sauce (F).

❼ Hang the chicken until the surface dries.

ROAST IN OVEN

❽ Remove hooks and roast in preheated to 200℃(400°F) for 30-35 minutes. Separate into wings, legs and breasts and carve into 2cm (1") slices to serve (G).

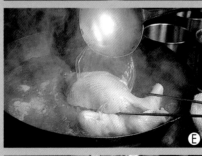

HELPFUL HINT

★ Rub ginger and green onion onto the inside and outside of chicken to give flavor.

Ingredients

4 servings

200 grams (7 oz) pork spareribs
1 tablespoon soy sauce
150 grams (5 oz) lotus root
Dash vinegar
1 tablespoon soy sauce
COOKING SAUCE
    1 tablespoon rice wine
    2 cups chicken stock

1 teaspoon sugar
1 tablespoon oyster sauce
1 tablespoon soy sauce
Pinch each MSG and pepper
1-2 tablespoons dissolved cornstarch
Komatsuna greens

Enjoy the full flavor of simmered sparerib.

SPARERIBS AND LOTUS ROOT

Directions

CUT INGREDIENTS

❶ Cut spareribs bone side down, into 3-4cm (1 1/4"-1 1/2") pieces (A).

❷ Coat spareribs with soy sauce (B).

❸ Skin lotus root and cut into 4-5cm(1 1/2"-2") lengths, then cut into 4 or 6 equal pieces.

❹ In a bowl add lotus root, dash of vinegar and water to cover completely; set aside to remove bitterness (C).

❺ Cook komatsuna in boiling water and drain. Cut into bite-size lengths.

STIR-FRY

❻ Heat wok until very hot and add vegetable oil. Place chicken and fry unstirred until lightly browned. Use a ladle to stir-fry (D).

❼ Drain excess oil through strainer (E).

SIMMER

❽ In a saucepan add spareribs and cooking sauce ingredients and simmer 40-50 minutes. Add lotus root and continue cooking for a further 15 minutes (F).

❾ Thicken the sauce with dissolved cornstarch to finish. Transfer to a serving dish and garnish with *komatsuna* greens.

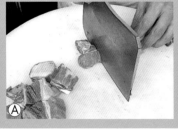   

HELPFUL HINT

★ Place spareribs bone side down when cutting. This makes cutting easier.

PROBLEMS TO AVOID

★ Do not lift the meat un browned, or it will stick the wok.

Ingredients ● 4 servings

1 (600 grams / 1 1/2 lbs) lobster
100 grams (3 1/3 oz) bean vermicelli
1 clove garlic
1 Belgian shallot
Cornstarch
Vegetable oil
Oil for deep-frying
1 tablespoon sa cha sauce
1 tablespoon rice wine
1 teaspoon hot bean paste
2 cups chicken stock
COOKING SAUCE
    1 tablespoon soy sauce
    1 teaspoon sugar
    Pinch MSG
    1 tablespoon oyster sauce
Prawns can be also used in place of lobster.

A moderately hot and spicy main course. Treat your guests to this attractive dish.

LOBSTER WITH BEAN VERMICELLI

● Directions ●

CUT INGREDIENTS

❶ Remove feelers from lobster and separate into head and body. Split in two lengthwise, then into bite-size pieces (A).

❷ Parboil bean vermicelli, drain and cut into bite-size lengths.

❸ Mince garlic and Belgian shallot and stir-fry in vegetable oil.

DEEP-FRY LOBSTER

❹ Dust lobster with cornstarch and deep-fry in 180℃(350°F) oil just until the coating becomes hard (B).

STIR-FRY AND BRAISE

❺ Heat wok until very hot and add vegetable oil, sa cha sauce, hot bean paste, garlic, shallot and rice wine. Stir-fry until the aroma is released (C).

❻ Pour in chicken stock and bring to the boil. Add lobster and bean vermicelli (D).

❼ Add cooking sauce ingredients and cook about 5 minutes (E).

HELPFUL HINT

★ Cornstarch coating will seal the flavor in during cooking.

CHEF'S SECRET

★ Save chicken skin in freezer. When there are enough to cook, add to boiling water to make stock.

● Directions ●

CUT INGREDIENTS

❶ Skin chicken breast and slice very thinly (A and B).

❷ In a bowl, place chicken and marinade ingredients; set aside (C).

❸ Cut Chinese broccoli in half, and cut the stalks into bite-size pieces.

❹ Slice green onion diagonally. Mince garlic and ginger.

STIR-FRY

❺ Heat wok until very hot and add vegetable oil. Briefly stir-fry Chinese broccoli and add salt and hot water to cook until soft; drain (D).

❻ Reheat the wok and add vegetable oil. Stir-fry chicken and stir in chili pepper, green onion, garlic and ginger (E).

❼ Add Chinese broccoli and season with pinch of salt, MSG, pepper and sesame oil (extra). Add sauce ingredients and thicken with dissolved cornstarch (G).

An appetizingly hot and spicy dish, a superb companion to cold beer.

CHICKEN AND CHINESE BROCCOLI

● Ingredients ● 4 servings

1 (200 grams / 7 oz) chicken breast
MARINADE
    Pinch each salt, MSG, and pepper
    Dash sesame oil
    1 teaspoon rice wine
    1/2 egg, lightly beaten
    1 teaspoon cornstarch
    1 tablespoon vegetable oil
200 grams (7 oz) Chinese broccoli
1/4 stalk green onion
1 clove garlic
1 small piece ginger
Vegetable oil
Pinch salt
1 teaspoon red chili pepper, sliced
COOKING SAUCE
    1/2 tablespoon each soy sauce and rice wine
    1/2 cup chicken stock
1 tablespoon dissolved cornstarch

Ingredients

4 servings

2 lily bulbs

250 grams(1/2 lb) shrimp

MARINADE

    Pinch each salt, MSG and pepper

    1 teaspoon rice wine

    Dash sesame oil

    1/2 egg white

    1 teaspoon baking soda

    2 teaspoons cornstarch

    1 tablespoon vegetable oil

1/4 each carrot and green onion

10 string beans

Vegetable oil

1/2 teaspoon each minced garlic and ginger

COOKING SAUCE

    1/2 tablespoon rice wine

    1/2 teaspoon soy sauce

    1/2 teaspoon oyster sauce

    Pinch each sugar, MSG and pepper

    1/4 cup chicken stock

2 tablespoons dissolved cornstarch

Lily bulb has a sweetish flavor which requires less seasonings. Parboil the bulbs for a speedy procedure.

SHRIMP AND LILY BULBS

Directions

CUT INGREDIENTS

❶ Wash lily bulbs in water to remove soil. Split in two and remove root (A).

❷ Peel off cloves from outside, cutting off the root if necessary (B).

❸ Shell shrimp and devein. Put in a bowl with marinade ingredients; set aside.

❹ Cut carrot into rolling wedges, string beans into 2 cm (3/4") lengths, and green onion into 1cm (3/8") slices.

PARBOIL

❺ Heat wok until very hot and add vegetable oil. Stir-fry shrimp until completely cooked. Drain oil through a strainer.

❻ In the same wok add lily bulbs and stir-fry. Pour in hot water and boil. Add string beans and carrot; drain in a colander(C and D).

STIR-FRY

❼ Reheat the wok, add vegetable oil, and stir-fry green onion, garlic and ginger. When the aroma is released, stir in shrimp and lily bulbs. Pour in chicken stock (E).

❽ Add cooking sauce ingredients and check the taste. Thicken the sauce with dissolved cornstarch (F).

HELPFUL HINT

★ Shake lily bulbs in a bowl of water to remove soil, changing the water several times.

● Ingredients ●   4 servings

8 chicken wing tips	1 teaspoon vegetable oil
SEASONING FOR CHICKEN	1 teaspoon rice wine
Pinch salt	1/3 cup chicken stock
Pinch MSG	COOKING SAUCE
Pinch pepper	2 teaspoon soy sauce
2 dried shiitake mushrooms, soaked in water	1 teaspoon oyster sauce
to soften	Pinch pepper
30 grams (1 oz) bamboo shoot	Oil for deep-frying
20 grams (2/3 oz) dried shark's fin, soaked in	Radish
water to soften	Leaf lettuce

Shark's fin sensation. Well absorbed seasonings increase the brilliancy of the food.

CHICKEN WING TIPS STUFFED WITH SHARK'S FIN

● Directions ●

PREPARE INGREDIENTS

❶ Fold ends of wing tips in the other way so the joints stick out. Using fingers, peel off flesh from the bone downwards and pull out the bone (A and B).

❷ Sprinkle with salt, MSG and pepper.

❸ Slice bamboo shoot and softened shiitake mushrooms thinly.

STIR-FRY

❹ Heat wok until very hot and add vegetable oil. Stir-fry shiitake mushrooms, bamboo shoot and pour in rice wine and chicken stock.

❺ Add drained shark's fin and cooking sauce. Reduce heat and continue to stir until shark's fin absorbs the flavor. Set aside to cool (C and D).

DEEP-FRY

❻ Stuff wing tips with shark's fin and secure the openings with toothpicks: Pierce a toothpick away from you, twist the chicken and pierce again in the same direction (E and F).

❼ In 150℃-160℃(300°F -325°F) oil, deep-fry stuffed chicken until golden brown; drain.

❽ Wrap the tips of chicken with aluminum foil several times to hold, and remove toothpicks (G).

❾ Arrange on a serving plate lined with leaf lettuce and garnish with radish.

Ⓐ

Ⓑ

Ⓒ

Ⓓ

(E) (F) (G)

↑ PROBLEMS TO AVOID

★ Stuff chicken with appropriate amount of shark's fin. Too much stuffing may cause a split in chicken when deep-fried.

↑ HELPFUL HINT

★ Remove toothpicks while hot. Aluminum foil wrapped around the ends will make holding the hot chicken much easier.

You'll be glad you had it!
Chinese Seasonings and Cooking Utensils

Before actual cooking , check if you have all the necessary seasonings and utensils. There are several items that are indispensable in Chinese cooking, e.g. wok and wok holder, hot bean paste and oyster sauce. These essentials will help you create authentic flavors. Start with a few basic items.

Cooking utensils

Wok

A multi-purpose pan with round bottom which conducts the heat evenly. A wok is ideal not only for stir-frying but deep-frying and simmering, or even for barbecueing meat and vegetables. Choose one made of carbon steel for good heat conduction, 28-30cm(11-12 inches) in diameter and with a single handle for easy maneuvering.

Wok strainer

A special strainer used to remove deep-fried food from oil at one time, and to blanch food in hot oil or water. Choose one which is slightly smaller than the wok. If not available, substitute with a single handle metal strainer.

Ladle

Perfect for stir-frying and braising any food in a wok. The preferred ladle has a sturdy joint and an easy-to-hold handle.

Wok holder

A ring to stabilize the wok when deep-frying. The round bottom of wok sits safely to prevent hot oil to spill out.

Steaming rack

An essential tool for steaming food, made of bamboo which allows steam rise efficiently. Place on a wok with boiling water as a single steamer or stack in several tiers so various dishes can be steamed at a time.

Chinese cleaver

A wide -bladed, heavy cleaver that facilitates cutting with its weight. The wide blade is useful for crushing fresh ginger, garlic or green onion. It takes some time to get used to the size, but is worth the effort. Can be used for intricate works.

Seasonings
The key to professional results

Oyster sauce

Salted and fermented oysters are matured and the top layer of the liquid makes the sauce. Its special aroma and subtle sweetness enhance the flavors of most dishes. Sprinkle a few drops over stir-fried iceberg lettuce, and you will love it.

Chicken stock granules

Instant chicken stock can be made with these by simply dissolving in hot water. As they contain more salt than you expect, reduce 20-30% of salt from the recipe, if using as a seasoning.

Chili oil

An orange color sesame oil in which red chili peppers have been soaked and removed. It is a must for jaozi, or Chinese dumplings, as a dipping sauce. Add a few drops to any salad dressing or sauce.

Black bean paste

Soft, black soy beans made from the process of fermentation, pickling in salt and sun-drying. Cut up and use to give a special flavor to stir-fried and simmered dishes.

Chinese wolfberry

Dried Chinese wolfberry originally and still used in Chinese medicine for its tonic action in liver and kidneys. Soak in rice wine to soften before cooking. Loved for the bright red appetizing color as well as for the sweet flavor.

Szechwan peppercorns

A refreshing fragrance of this spice is favored also for its odor-killing effect on meats. Similar to *Sansho* pepper of Japan, but has a sharper pungency which is a must for Szechwan Mapo *tofu*.

Shaosing wine

Chinese rice wine enjoyed as a drink and as a seasoning. Small amount of shaohsing wine adds a mild flavor while removing the smell of meats. Dry sherry can be an alternative.

Five-spice powder

An aromatic blend of five oriental spices: Szechwan pepper (fagaro), cinnamon, cloves, dried mandarin peel, and star anise or fennel. Enhance the flavors of meats and seafood.

XO sauce

A rich, concentrated sauce made from dried shrimp, dried scallops, garlic, red chili pepper, etc. Gives a flavorful aroma to most stir-fried dishes including fried rice and fried noodles.

Baking soda

Helps to cook soy beans soft, and to tenderize beef if added in the marinade. It also works to prevent frozen seafood from becoming soft and soggy.

Coriander

Known as cilantro or Chinese parsley, fresh coriander often garnishes Chinese dishes as well as Mexican or other Asian dishes except Japanese and Korean. The seeds are dried and ground to be used as a spice.

Sesame paste

White sesame seeds ground and blended with sesame seed oil. Its rich and aromatic flavor give a deeper flavor to food as in Pang Pang Chicken, or chicken salad.

Sa cha sauce

A spicy paste based on ten men jiang, a Chinese fermented bean paste. Garlic, fennel, chili pepper, and five-spice powder are added to the paste. Good for sautéed meats.

Sesame oil

Clear brown oil with a distinct nutty taste and fragrant aroma. A few drops will enchance any stir-fried dishes.

Hot bean paste

Steamed broad beans are fermented with chili pepper, salt, oil and malted rice to make a very hot and slightly salty paste. Often used in northern cuisine for stir-frying dishes and dressings. Stir-fry well until the spicy aroma is extracted.

Dried shrimp

This is an important Chinese ingredient and it creates utterly different flavor from the fresh one. Shell and soak in water and then use in soups or stir-fried dishes to give a mild, savory flavor.

Softening dried shrimp:

Soak in warmed chicken stock or water until soft for about 30 minutes. The soaking liquid can be used as a stock.

Dried scallops

Great for soups, simmering dishes and porridges. Soaking water itself makes a delicate, flavorful stock.

Softening dried scallops:

Soak in warmed chicken stock or water until soft. Can be put into cold water and immediately steamed to soften. Use the soaking water as a delicate stock.

Rices, Noodles, and Soups

Unique one dish rice or noodle meal which contains carbohydrate, protein, and minerals of vegetables . Add a bowl of soup and the dinner will be perfect. Once you learn the basic recipes, variations are countless using different ingredients and seasonings.

200 grams (7 oz) thinly sliced pork
MARINADE
    Pinch each salt, MSG, pepper
    1 teaspoon rice wine
    1 teaspoon soy sauce
    1 teaspoon sesame oil
    1/2 egg, lightly beaten
    1 tablespoon cornstarch
    1 tablespoon vegetable oil
150 grams (5 oz) shrimp
MARINADE
    Pinch each salt, MSG and pepper
    1 teaspoon rice wine
    Dash sesame oil
    1 tablespoon egg white
    1/3 teaspoon cornstarch
    1 tablespoon vegetable oil
2 Chinese cabbage leaves

20 grams (2/3 oz) carrot, cut into
    rectangles
50 grams (1 2/3 oz) bamboo shoot,
    thinly sliced
4 dried shiitake mushrooms, softened
20 snow peas, strung
4 portions Chinese noodles
Salad oil
COOKING SAUCE
    1 tablespoon rice wine
    2 cups chicken stock
    3 tablespoons soy sauce
    1 teaspoon Chinese soy sauce
    Dash MSG, sugar and pepper
3 tablespoons dissolved cornstarch
Dash sesame oil

CHEF'S SECRET

★ Leave some space in center so the steam circulates in the steamer for an even cooking.

Crisp fried noodles contrast well with the plentiful ingredients in a thick and smooth sauce.

MIXED FRIED NOODLES

● **Directions** ●

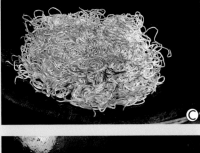

CUT INGREDIENTS

❶ Cut pork slices into bite-size pieces and put in the marinade; set aside. Shell and devein shrimp, then marinade.

❷ Cut up Chinese cabbage; cut white stalks at a slant to enlarge the cut edges, and cut leaves into large pieces. Cut softened shiitake into bite-size pieces.

STEAM AND FRY NOODLES

❸ In a boiling steamer, place noodles separating with fingers and forming a ring. Steam about 8-10 minutes (A and B).

❹ Heat the wok very hot and add vegetable oil. Add cooked noodles spreading evenly. When the bottom of noodles is browned turn over and cook; place on a serving plate (C).

STIR-FRY TOPPING

❺ Add vegetable oil to the wok and stir-fry pork, then shrimp (D).

❻ Add Chinese cabbage, carrot, bamboo shoot and *shiitake* mushrooms in the order and stir-fry. Add cooking sauce (E).

❼ When the Chinese cabbage is soft, stir in snow peas and cook briefly. Stir in dissolved cornstarch and thicken the sauce (F).

❽ Finish by sprinkling sesame oil and pour on top of the noodles.

Ingredients · 4 servings

4 portions Chinese noodles
200 grams (7 oz) thinly sliced pork
MARINADE
    Pinch each salt, MSG and pepper
    1 teaspoon each rice wine and soy sauce
    Dash sesame oil
    1/4 egg, lightly beaten
    1 teaspoon cornstarch
    1 tablespoon vegetable oil
400 grams (13 oz) bean sprouts
2 packages enokitake mushrooms
4 dried shiitake mushrooms, softened
1/4 medium carrot
100 grams (3 1/3 oz) komatuna greens
1 tablespoon vegetable oil
COOKING SAUCE
    Pinch each salt, pepper and MSG
    4 tablespoons oyster sauce
    2 tablespoons vegetable oil
    1 1/2 tablespoons Worcester sauce

The popular stall noodles can turn into a restaurant quality dinner with a little technique.

STIR-FRIED NOODLES

Directions

STEAM AND FRY NOODLES

❶ Cook noodles as for page 75.

CUT INGREDIENTS

❷ Cut pork into julienne strips and mix with the marinade; set aside.

❸ Discard the root ends of enokitake mushrooms and cut in half. Cut softened shiitake mushrooms and carrot into julienne strips. Cut komatuna into 4-5cm (2") lengths.

STIR-FRY

❹ Heat wok until very hot and add vegetable oil. Briefly stir-fry vegetables and pour in hot water. Cook 1-2 minutes and drain (A).

❺ Clean and reheat the wok. Add vegetable oil and stir-fry pork strips until well done. Add noodles and stir-fry, separating with chopsticks.

❼ Stir in vegetables and add cooking sauce (B and C).

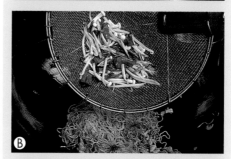

CHEF'S SECRET

★ Oyster sauce plays an important role in this recipe. Its rich flavor and subtle sweetness upgrades the taste.

HELPFUL HINT

★ If steaming process is too much work, cook chicken in simmering water, remove and add marinade ingredients except water.

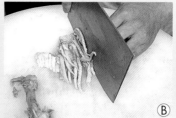

CHEF'S SECRET

★ A few drops of soy sauce will add a pleasant aroma to salt-based soup like this.

Directions

MAKE STEAMED CHICKEN

❶ Season chicken legs and steam in a steamer. When fully cooked, place in the marinade skin side down and let stand at least 1 hour (A).

❷ Debone chicken and cut into julienne strips (B).

❸ Cook noodles in boiling water to your favorite doneness; remove and drain.

❹ In the same wok cook komatsuna and blanch in cold water; drain and cut into 4-5 cm (2") lengths. Slice green onion (C).

❺ In a serving bowl, combine soup ingredients (D).

❻ Put cooked noodles arranging neatly with chopsticks. Top with chicken and vegetables.

CHICKEN NOODLES

Ingredients   4 servings

2 chicken legs
SEASONINGS FOR CHICKEN
    1/3 teaspoon salt
    Pinch MSG
    Szechwan peppercorn
MARINADE
    3 cups hot water
    5 cm (2 ") green onion
    1 small piece fresh ginger
    Pinch each salt, MSG and pepper
    1 tablespoon rice wine
    Dash sesame oil
SOUP
    1/4 teaspoon salt
    2 teaspoons MSG
    Dash sesame oil
    Dash pepper
    2 teaspoons soy sauce
    6 cups chicken stock
4 portions Chinese noodles
Komatuna greens and green onion

Ingredients ● 4 servings

30 grams(1 oz) dried shrimp

100 grams (3 1/3 oz) Szechwan pickle

1 stalk green onion

1 bunch garlic chives

150 grams(5 oz) minced pork

4 portions Chinese noodles

1 tablespoon each vegetable oil and hot bean
  paste

4 tablespoons sesame paste

1 tablespoon rice wine

6 cups chicken stock

1 tablespoon soy sauce

Pinch each salt, MSG, pepper

Dash sesame oil

Favorite spicy noodles with a balanced spiciness.
Once you try, you won't be able to resist it.

HOT & SPICY NOODLES

● Directions ●

CUT INGREDIENTS

❶ Soak dried shrimp in lukewarm water or chicken stock (A).

❷ Mince Szechwan pickle and soak in water to reduce saltiness. Slice green onion and cut garlic chives into 2cm(1 ") lengths (B).

COOK NOODLES

❸ In wok bring water to the boil and cook separated noodles to your liking (C).

❹ Drain noodles in a strainer and transfer to a serving bowl (D).

STIR-FRY TOPPING

❺ Reheat the wok and add vegetable oil. Stir-fry dried shrimp, and add minced pork. When the pork is thoroughly cooked, stir in hot bean paste. Continue stirring (E).

❻ Stir in sesame paste and a little shrimp-soaking water carefully. Gradually thin the paste with remaining soaking water (F).

❼ Add Szechwan pickle, green onion and garlic chives and keep stirring. Pour in rice wine, chicken stock and soy sauce. Season with salt, MSG and pepper. Bring to boil and cook a further 3-4 minutes without stirring. Sprinkle with sesame oil.

❽ Pour over the cooked noodles.

CHEF'S SECRET

★ Hot bean paste must be stir-fried well enough to extract the flavor before adding food.

HELPFUL HINT

★ Braise for a while at this stage, and the ingredients will give off the best flavors.

79

Ingredients 4 servings

6 cups chicken stock

20 grams (2/3 oz) kombu kelp

10 grams (1/3 oz) dried bonito shavings

1/2 stalk green onion

400 grams(1 1/3 oz) somen noodles

1 tablespoon soy sauce

Pinch pepper

1 tablespoon dissolved cornstarch

Dash sesame oil

Fresh coriander and hot bean paste

Japanese dashi stock is added to chicken stock to create a flavorful soup for the delicate noodles.

SOMEN IN THICK SOUP

 Directions

MAKE DASHI STOCK

❶ In wok add cold chicken stock and kombu kelp. Just before the boiling point, take out kombu.

❷ Add dried bonito shavings and cook 1 minute; remove from heat and let stand until the bonito shavings settle on the bottom. Strain and set aside (A).

COOL NOODLES

❸ Cut green onion into 5 cm (2") length, then into shreds. Blanch in cold water (B).

❹ Bring a large amount of water to the boil. Add somen noodles and cook just until it becomes supple about 1 minute; drain (C and D).

COOK IN DASHI STOCK

❺ Bring dashi stock to the boil and add somen. When the somen is soft season with soy sauce and pepper. Thicken the stock with dissolved cornstarch (E).

❻ Sprinkle with sesame oil and pour into a serving bowl. Top with drained green onion , coriander and hot bean paste.

HELPFUL HINT

★ If using chicken stock granules, put kombu in water and bring to the boil, remove kombu and combine with the granules and dried bonito flakes.

Ⓐ

Ⓑ

Ⓒ

Ⓓ

Ⓔ

CHEF'S SECRET

★ Do not overcook somen since it cooks in only a few minutes.

Braised Pork Rice

🔴 Ingredients 🔴 4 servings

2 cloves garlic

1 stalk green onion

4 dried shiitake mushrooms, softened

300 grams (10 oz) minced pork

1 tablespoon each vegetable oil and rice wine

2 cups chicken stock

2 tablespoons soy sauce

Dash oyster sauce and pepper

8 quail eggs

Steamed rice

🔴 Directions 🔴

CUT AND STIR-FRY

❶ Cut up garlic and green onion. Cut drained *shiitake* mushrooms into 1cm cubes.

❷ Heat wok until very hot and add vegetable oil. Stir-fry garlic and green

HELPFUL HINT

★ It is hard to prevent burdock from discoloring, but by adding some soy sauce it will be camouflaged.

Egg and Burdock Soup

🔴 Ingredients 🔴 4 servings

1/2 burdock

1/2 carrot

2 dried shiitake mushroom

1 tablespoon each sesame oil and rice wine

4 cups chicken stock

2 tablespoons soy sauce

2 eggs, lightly beaten

CHEF'S SECRET

★ The longer the meat is cooked, the more flavorful and tenderer. Simmer 40 minutes to 1 hour if possible.

onion (A).

❸ Add minced meat and stir well until cooked. Drizzle in rice wine from the sides of wok, then pour in stock (B).

❹ Bring to the boil and add soy sauce, oyster sauce and pepper. Add *shiitake* mushrooms and quail eggs. Cook covered over low heat at least 20 minutes (C and D).

❺ Place on top of hot steaming rice.

🔵 Directions 🔵

CUT INGREDIENTS

❶ Peel burdock rubbing with the blunt edge of cleaver. Cut into fine julienne strips and blanch in water to remove harshness.

❷ Cut carrot into fine julienne strips. Soften dried *shiitake* mushroom in water and cut into fine julienne strips.

STIR-FRY

❸ Heat wok until very hot. Add vegetable oil and stir-fry burdock, then carrot and mushrooms.

❹ Add rice wine and chicken stock. Season with salt, MSG, and soy sauce (E).

❺ Stir in beaten eggs and when they are almost cooked, remove from heat.

Slowly braised minced meat goes perfectly well with hot rice and light soup.

BRAISED PORK RICE WITH EGG AND BURDOCK SOUP

● **Ingredients** ● 4 servings

6 dried scallops

1 cup rice

1 tablespoon vegetable oil

3 liters (1/4 gallon) water

1 salt-preserved egg

8 small fillets white meat fish

40 grams (1 1/3 oz) shrimp

SEASONINGS FOR SEAFOOD

    Salt, MSG, pepper, rice wine, sesame oil, egg white, baking soda, cornstarch and vegetable oil

50 grams (1 2/3 oz)Szechwan pickle

20 grams (2/3 oz) Chinese greens

CONDIMENTS

    Green onion, coriander, fried wonton skin and fermented tofu

SAUCE

    Soy sauce and chili oil

Enjoy the variety of fine toppings. The rice is cooked with dried scallops which make a delicate broth.

RICE PORRIDGE WITH DRIED SCALLOPS

● **Directions** ●

COOK RICE

❶ Soak dried scallops in warmed chicken stock or hot water and set aside until soft; break up into small pieces (A).

❷ Wash rice and drain. Stir in vegetable oil and let stand 30-60 minutes (B and C).

❸ In wok add water, rice, softened scallops and the soaking water. Cover and cook over medium heat (D and E).

❹ Bring to the boil, then reduce heat and cook uncovered 5-6 hours (F).

PREPARE TOPPINGS

❺ Shell preserved egg and cut into halves. Cook seasoned white fish and shrimp and in boiling water.

❻ Slice Szechwan pickle thinly and soak in water to remove extra saltiness. Cook Chinese greens in boiling water and cut into 4-5cm(2") pieces.

❼ Finely shred green onion. Strip off coriander leaves.

SERVE

❽ Place rice porridge in a serving bowl and place toppings on a serving plate. Serve with small plates of condiments so everyone can take his choice.

Ⓐ

Ⓑ

Ⓒ

HELPFUL HINT

★ By adding a tablespoon of vegetable oil to the water, the cooked rice will not get too sticky or scorch at the bottom.

Richly flavored steamed rice with light soup.

STEAMED RICE WITH LILY BUD SOUP

Steamed Rice with Chinese Sausage

● Ingredients ●   4 servings

3 cups rice
3 cups water
1 Chinese sausage
2 dried shiitake mushrooms, softened
20 grams (2/3 oz) bamboo shoot
20 grams (2/3 oz) dried shrimp, softened

1 tablespoon vegetable oil
1/2 tablespoon rice wine
1 tablespoon shrimp soaking water
SEASONINGS
   2 tablespoons soy sauce
   Salt and pepper
   1 teaspoon sesame oil

● Directions ●

RINSE RICE AND CUT INGREDIENTS

❶ Rinse rice in cold water and drain 30-60 minutes.

❷ Soak dried mushrooms and shrimp in lukewarm water. Dice sausage, mushrooms and bamboo shoot into the same size (A).

COOK INGREDIENTS AND ADD TO RICE

❸ Heat wok until very hot. Add vegetable oil and stir-fry sausage and shrimp. When the aroma is released, add mushrooms and bamboo shoot and stir-fry well (B).

❹ Add rice wine and shrimp soaking water. Season with soy sauce, salt and pepper, and sesame oil. Transfer to a bowl and let stand to cool.

❺ In a rice cooker, lightly mix rice, water and the cooled ingredients. Turn on the cooker. When cooked, fluff rice to mix the ingredients evenly (C).

Lily Bud Soup

● Ingredients ●   4 servings

20 grams (2/3 oz) dried lily buds
100 grams (3 1/3 oz) thinly sliced pork
10 grams (1/3 oz) cloud ear fungi
20 grams (2/3 oz) bamboo shoot
1 tablespoon vegetable oil
1 tablespoon rice wine
6 cups chicken stock
Pinch each salt, MSG
Dash sesame oil

● Directions ●

CUT INGREDIENTS

❶ Soak dried lily buds in lukewarm water. Trim by cutting off hard bottoms. Tie each bud into a knot (D and E).

❷ Cut pork into julienne strips and cook in boiling water; drain. Soak cloud ears in hot water. Cut cloud ears and bamboo shoot into julienne strips.

HEAT THEM

❸ In well-heated wok add vegetable oil and pour in rice wine and chicken stock. Add lily buds and cook until soft.

❹ Add pork, cloud ears and bamboo shoot and bring to the boil. Season with salt and MSG. Skim the foam and sprinkle with sesame oil before serving (F).

Ⓐ

Ⓑ

Ⓒ

HELPFUL HINT

★ Lily buds are tied into knots to prevent them from opening wide when simmered.

Ⓓ

Ⓔ

Ⓕ

PROBLEMS TO AVOID

★ Be sure to use warm rice. If cold rice is used, the heat of the wok will draw out the moisture of the rice and the whole thing will become sticky.

CHEF'S SECRET

★ It is most recommendable to cook fried rice in a small portion at a time. Divide 4 servings in half and cook twice for the best result.

● Directions ●

PREPARE INGREDIENTS

❶ Shred Chinese pickled greens and soak in water 3 minutes to remove extra saltiness. Drain and squeeze tightly (A).

❷ Heat wok until very hot. Add vegetable oil and briefly stir-fry dried young sardines; drain (B).

STIR-FRY

❸ Add more oil and pour in beaten eggs. Quickly stir-fry (C).

❹ When the eggs are almost cooked, add hot cooked rice and stir-fry, separating rice grains (D).

❺ Add young sardines and stir-fry well. Check the taste and season with salt, MSG and pepper (E).

❻ Drizzle in soy sauce from the sides of wok to give an aroma to rice (F).

A basic fried rice featuring the salty pickles. Sprinkle with soy sauce for the finishing touch.

FRIED RICE WITH PICKLED GREENS

● Ingredients ● 4 servings

100 grams (3 1/3 oz) Szechwan pickle

50 grams (1 2/3 oz) dried young sardines

Vegetable oil

4 eggs, lightly beaten

1 kilo grams (2 1/4 lb) cooked rice

Pinch each salt, MSG

Pinch pepper

Dash soy sauce

Ingredients ● 4 servings

100 grams (3 1/3 oz) fresh sea slug
1/2 cake tofu
1/4 carrot
2 dried shiitake mushrooms, softened
1/4 green onion
2 egg whites, lightly beaten
6 cups chicken stock
Pinch salt, and MSG and pepper
2 tablespoons soy sauce
3 tablespoons dissolved cornstarch
3 tablespoons rice vinegar
Chili oil

Pungent pepper and chili oil teamed with vinegar make a lighter, mild dish that stimulates your appetite.

HOT AND SOUR SOUP

● Directions ●

CUT INGREDIENTS

❶ Cook sea slug in boiling water and cut into bite-size pieces. Cut tofu into 1cm (3/8") cubes, carrot into thin half moons, shiitake and green onion into 1.5cm (1/2") squares (A).

BRAISE

❷ Add chicken stock to wok and cook all ingredients except sea slug over medium low heat (B).

❸ When the tofu is cooked season with salt, MSG, soy sauce, and ample pepper. Stir in dissolved cornstarch to thicken the sauce (C).

❹ When the liquid is bubbling, drizzle in egg white in a large, circular motion. When the egg whites are set, stir in rice vinegar. Sprinkle with chili oil (D).

CHEF'S SECRET

★ The basic seasonings for soup should be salt and MSG. Check the taste at this stage and add other seasonings as needed.

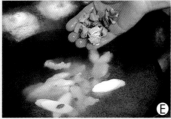

CHEF'S SECRET

★ Enjoy the harmony of gourmet's delights. Available in Oriental food shops.

HELPFUL HINT

★ Seal the casserole with plastic wrap in order to prevent water dripping into the edges of the lid.

● Directions ●

PREPARE INGREDIENTS

❶ Dice Chinese ham. Cook soaked shark's fin in boiling water until soft. Soak dried scallops in lukewarm water, dried mushrooms in water, Chinese wolfberries in rice wine until soft (A).

❷ In wok heat oil for frying to about 80℃(175°F) and deep-fry fish bladder slowly until the transparency is gone. Drain, soak in lukewarm water about 1 hour, and cut into bite-size pieces (B)

❸ Deep-fry Achilles' tendons at about 80℃(175°F) 15-20 minutes until white and swollen; drain and soak in lukewarm water about 40 minutes (C and D)

❹ Cook chicken in boiling water.

BOIL IN STOCK, AND STEAM

❺ In wok bring chicken stock to the boil and add all ingredients except chicken. Cook about 10 minutes and season with salt and pepper (E).

❻ In a casserole, place chicken and other cooked ingredients. Put the lid on and cover entirely with plastic wrap.

❼ In a steaming, deep steamer put the casserole and steam 5-6 hours, adding hot water occasionally.

A dainty soup using all Chinese delicacies, to appreciate both the ingredients and the broth.

Heavenly Soup

● Ingredients ● 4 servings

100 grams (3 1/3 oz) Chinese ham

50 grams (1 2/3 oz) dried shark's fin, soaked in water

8 dried scallops

8 dried shiitake mushrooms

10 grams (1/3 oz) Chinese wolfberries

50 grams (1 2/3 oz) dried Chinese yam

50 grams (1 2/3 oz) dried air bladder of fish

40 grams (1 1/3 oz) dried pig's Achilles' tendons

Oil for deep-frying

1 whole chicken

7 cups of chicken stock

Salt and pepper

Dim Sum and Desserts

Dim sum not only includes the popular dumplings such as siu mai but the sweet desserts to complete the meal. They are fun to cook and eat as well. Cook for everyday meal or make a variety for a dim sum party!

● Ingredients ●   Yields 12

200 grams (7 oz) cabbage
Pinch salt
30 grams (1 oz) garlic chives
100 grams (3 1/3 oz) minced pork
SEASONINGS
    Pinch each salt and MSG

2 tablespoons soy sauce
1 tablespoon rice wine
1 teaspoon shaohsing wine
1 teaspoon sesame oil
Pinch pepper
1 teaspoon lard

1/2 teaspoon each minced garlic
    and fresh ginger
12 jiaozi skins
Vegetable oil
Parsley

HELPFUL HINT

★ It is better to shred the cabbage as finely as possible before chopping because too much chopping will spoil the flavor.

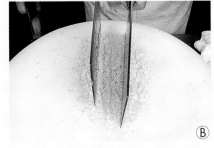

Exquisite balance between the crisp outside and juicy dumpling inside! "Kneading" the meat is the key to a professional taste.

FRIED JIAOZI(Fried Dumplings)

● **Directions** ●

CUT INGREDIENTS

❶ Cut cabbage into fine shreds, and then mince. Chop again using two cleavers (A and B).

❷ In a bowl add cabbage and salt. Mix in rubbing motion and tightly squeeze out moisture (C and D).

❸ Mince garlic chives.

"KNEAD" MEAT

❹ In another bowl put minced pork and seasonings. Using your fingers mix well until the meat turns whitish and sticky (E and F).

❺ Combine cabbage and garlic chives. Add this to the meat and mix evenly. Keep in refrigerator about half an hour (G).

WRAP IN SKIN AND FRY

❻ On a sheet of jiaozi skin place a dab of meat mixture. Wet the edges of skin and pinch one end (H).

❼ Fold the pushed out upper skin forming a pleat. Repeat in the same manner towards the other end.

❽ Heat wok until very hot. Add vegetable oil and fry the bottoms of jiaozi until brown. Pour in about a half cup of water and cover at once; cook until the liquid is gone (H).

❾ Remove the lid to release extra moisture. Transfer to a serving plate and garnish with parsley. (Serve with dipping sauce.)

CHEF'S SECRET

★ Flatten the meat surface and hold the skin of your side at a right angle to the other half. This way you can wrap jiaozi easily.

Enjoy the soft and savory ingredients inside the crisp fried skin.

SPECIAL SPRING ROLLS

● Ingredients ●   Yields 4

2 dried shiitake mushrooms, softened
30 grams (1 oz) bamboo shoot
20 grams (2/3 oz) bean sprouts
50 grams (1 2/3 oz) thinly sliced pork
SEASONINGS FOR PORK
    Pinch salt, MSG, pepper, rice wine, soy
    sauce, sesame oil, beaten egg, cornstarch and
    vegetable oil
50 grams (1 2/3 oz) shrimp
SEASONINGS FOR SHRIMP
    Pinch salt, MSG, pepper, rice wine, sesame
    oil, egg white, baking soda, cornstarch and
    vegetable oil
COOKING SAUCE
    1 tablespoon rice wine
    1/3 cup chicken stock
    1 tablespoon each soy sauce and oyster sauce
    Pinch each sugar, MSG and pepper
1 1/2 tablespoons dissolved cornstarch
Sesame oil
8 spring roll wrappers
Oil for deep-frying
Cabbage, carrot and parsley
Tomato ketchup and mustard

● Directions ●

CUT INGREDIENTS

❶ Shred mushrooms and bamboo shoot. Cook bean sprouts in boiling water and drain. Shred pork slices and add seasonings. Slice shrimp into 1cm (3/8") and add seasonings (A).

STIR-FRY

❷ Heat wok until very hot. Add vegetable oil and stir-fry pork until the color changes. Stir in shrimp, mushrooms and bamboo shoot. Lastly add bean sprouts (B).

❸ Stir in cooking sauce ingredients. Thicken the sauce with cornstarch and sprinkle with sesame oil; let stand to cool (C).

WRAP AND DEEP-FRY

❹ Lay a spring roll wrapper on the point and place 1/8 portion of the stuffing.   Bring up the corner, fold up the sides and roll away from you (D).

❺ Secure the end corner with moistened flour and set aside, rolled end down. Make 8 rolls (E).

❻ Heat oil to 180℃(175°F) and deep-fry the rolls until crisp; drain (F).

❼ Place on a serving plate and garnish with parsley, shredded cabbage and carrot. Serve with tomato ketchup, mustard or relishes of your choice.

HELPFUL HINT

★ Put wrapped rolls, ends down, and the weight of the rolls will help them stick well.

HELPFUL HINT

★ Cut shrimp and pork into almost the same size so the mixing will be easier.

(A)

(B)

(C)

(D)

(E)

(F)

Directions

CUT INGREDIENTS

❶ Chop softened mushrooms and green onions coarsely. Cut shrimp into 1 cm (3/8") pieces. Shred pork slices, then chop (A).

COMBINE INGREDIENTS

❷ In a bowl combine pork, shrimp and marinade ingredients and mix well until sticky (B).

❸ In the same bowl place green onions and mushrooms, coat with cornstarch so each piece separates. Combine with pork and shrimp (C).

WRAP AND STEAM

❹ In the center of the siu mai skin place a dab of meat mixture and bring up the sides. Press the top and bottom into shape (D and E).

❺ Place in a steamer and steam about 15 minutes. Transfer to a serving dish and garnish with parsley. Serve with mustard and soy sauce (F).

Cut ingredients coarsely for an enjoyable bite on the juicy siu mai. Serve piping hot.

SHIITAKE AND PORK SIU MAI

● **Ingredients** ● Yields 16

2-3 dried shiitake mushrooms, softened

2 green onions

50 grams (1 2/3 oz) shrimp

300 grams(10 oz) sliced pork

MARINADE

    1 teaspoon or less salt

    1 teaspoon MSG

    1 tablespoon sugar

    1 1/3 tablespoons soy sauce

    1 tablespoon sesame oil

Cornstarch

16 siu mai skins

Parsley

Mr Hideo Iwasa, Seiko-en Shinkan, who instructed helping Tomiteru Shu.

Ingredients   Yields 8

200 grams (7 oz) refined rice flour

50 grams (1 2/3 oz) sugar

2 tablespoons custard powder

1 cup water

40 grams (1 1/3 oz) wheat starch

15 grams (1/2 oz) lard

1/3 cup boiling water

200g (7 oz) bean jam

50g (1 2/3 oz) sesame seeds, ground

White sesame seeds

Oil for deep-frying

A popular Chinese sweet dim sum to go with tea. Serve piping hot to enjoy the tempting aroma of sesame seeds and subtle custard flavor.

FRIED SESAME BALLS

Directions

MAKE A DOUGH

❶ In a bowl add refined rice flour, sugar, and custard powder. Add water, saving some for later (A).

❷ Knead with strength, until no lumps of flour are seen (B).

❸ In another bowl add wheat starch and lard. Pour in boiling water. Using a pestle, press down to mix. Then knead with your hand (C and D).

❹ Add this to the bowl of rice flour mixture and knead again, pressing down with the heel of your hand. Gradually add the remaining water and knead until smooth and pliable (E).

SHAPE INTO BALLS

❺ Mix bean jam and ground sesame seeds well and shape into 1.5cm (1/2") balls.

❻ Take some dough, a little larger than the table tennis ball, and shape into a ball. Flatten between your palms and center the jam ball. Wrap up and reshape (F). Make 8 balls.

❼ In a bat filled with white sesame seeds, roll the balls until completely coated with the seeds (G).

DEEP-FRY

❽ Heat oil to 130-140℃(260-275°F) and turn off the heat. Slide in the balls and deep-fry unheated, occasionally stirring to prevent sticking to the bottom of wok. When the balls rise to the surface of oil, turn the heat on and deep-fry until golden (H).

❾ Drain on a strainer.

HELPFUL HINT

★ The dough can be light and sticky at this stage.

PROBLEMS TO AVOID

★ Press sesame seeds to secure, or they well splash away when deep-fried.

Ingredients 4 servings

3 cups coconut milk

3 cups milk

130 grams (4 1/3 oz) sugar

3 cups water

20 grams (2/3 oz) azuki beans, soaked overnight
    in water

20 grams (2/3 oz) sweet potato

50 grams (1 2/3 oz) tapioca pearls

Green tea powder

You will say you have another stomach saved
for this dessert after a big meal. A Japanese
version of coconut milk with tapioca.

COCONUT MILK
JAPANESE STYLE

 Directions

HEAT COCONUT MILK

❶ In a saucepan add coconut milk, milk, sugar
and water. Bring to the boil and remove from
heat. Set aside to cool (A and B).

PREPARE INGREDIENTS

❷ Boil drained azuki beans over low heat until
soft; drain and cool. Dice peeled sweet potato
into 5mm (1/4") and blanch in water, then boil
and drain. Set aside to cool.

❸ Cook tapioca pearls in boiling water 10
minutes; drain and let stand to cool.

❹ Dissolve green tea powder in a little water.

SERVE

❺ Take half amount of coconut milk mixture and
stir in dissolved green tea until it has the color
of your taste. Mix half of tapioca pearls and
diced sweet potato. Mix remaining coconut
milk mixture, remaining tapioca and azuki
beans (C).

❻ Refrigerate well and serve with a spoon.

HELPFUL HINT

★ Heat just until the sugar
dissolves.

PROBLEMS TO AVOID

★Be sure to whip egg whites stiff, or the "snow" will look soggy.

● Directions ●

WHIP EGG WHITES

❶ In a bowl, whip egg whites adding sugar several times until a stiff peak is formed when the whisk is lifted (A).

MAKE JELLY BASE

❷ In a small saucepan add water and agar agar. Bring to the boil and stir until agar agar dissolves.

❸ In a bowl combine egg yolks and condensed milk. Add dissolved agar agar and stir well (B and C).

STEAM

❹ Add jelly base gradually to egg whites and fold gently. Pour in serving glasses and steam 20 minutes (D).

❺ Refrigerate at least 30-40 minutes before serving.

Fluffy, creamy pudding just melts in your mouth! An elegant, jellied custard with meringue.

SNOW-TOPPED PUDDING

● **Ingredients** ● 4 servings

2 eggs, separated

20 grams (2/3 oz) sugar

5 tablespoons condensed milk

4 grams (1/8 oz) powdered agar agar

1 cups water

Ingredients 4 servings

1 papaya
5 cups milk
Sugar according to your taste
200 grams (7 oz) frozen green peas
Honey

Healthy milk shakes with digestive fruit and vegetable. Add to your breakfast menu as an energy source!

PAPAYA MILK SHAKE GREEN PEA MILK SHAKE

Directions

PUT IN BLENDER

❶ Cut papaya in half and remove seeds. Scoop out the flesh (A and B).

❷ In a blender or food processor, blend papaya and half amount of milk. Check the taste and add sugar, if desired (C).

❸ Skin green peas and put in the blender. Pour in remaining milk and honey and blend well.

❹ Refrigerate before serving.

Ⓐ

Ⓑ

Ⓒ

Add honey for a better flavor as green peas are not sweet enough.

HELPFUL HINT

★ In summer, chill glasses.

PROBLEMS TO AVOID

★ Add sugar after the gelatin is dissolved, or the sugar will bring down the temperature and prevent dissolving.

 Directions

MAKE JELLY BASE

❶ Soak powdered gelatin in double amount of water.

❷ In wok add water and powdered agar agar and bring to the boil. When the agar agar is dissolved, remove from heat and add gelatin and sugar (A).

❸ Stir in condensed milk, then almond water. Stir well (B and C).

❹ In a bowl add milk, and pour in the jelly base straining through a sieve. Mix lightly and skim the foam (D and E).

❺ When slightly cooled, refrigerate until set.

MAKE SYRUP AND SERVE

❻ In a saucepan bring water to the boil and add sugar. When the sugar is dissolved, remove from heat and stir in lemon juice. Chill in the refrigerator.

❼ Using a large slotted spoon, scoop thin layers of jelly and place in a serving bowl. Pour syrup over the jelly and decorate with fruits.

 Ingredients 4 servings

1 cup water
3 grams (1/8 oz) powdered agar agar
3 grams (1/8 oz) powdered gelatin
30 grams (1 oz) sugar
2 tablespoons condensed milk
1 teaspoon almond water
1 1/2 cups milk
SYRUP
    3 cups water
    80 grams (2 2/3 oz) sugar
    Lemon juice
Fruits of your choice

Ingredients for almond jelly. Almond water, the key source of the flavor, is available at Oriental drugstores.

A popular Chinese dessert, favored for its smooth and light texture. Chill well and present like layers of white clouds.

ALMOND JELLY

GETTING TO KNOW YOUR WOK

The wok is the all-purpose cooking pot.

The traditional form of Chinese wok is a round or flat-bottomed pot made of heavy gauge carbon steel. The most common Oriental cooking methods include stir-frying, deep-frying, simmering, boiling, and steaming. Depending upon the method utilized, ingredients generally retain their natural flavor and nutrition with new and different tastes emerging from the use of each method.

Stir-Frying	*Steaming*	*Simmering*	*Deep-Frying*	*Boiling*

WOK WITH ONE HANDLE

The wok is deep, like a soup pot, so you can boil rice and make soup in it. The wok's rounded sides provide enough red-hot surface for stir-frying foods quickly, usually in 3 to 5 minutes. The wok with one handle is easy to move over high heat with one hand while you add new ingredients and stir with the other hand. Stir-frying cooks protein foods thoroughly while at the same time leaving them tender and juicy and vegetables retain the intense color and crisp texture.

The modern wok is made of lightweight stainless steel or aluminum with one or two handles. Also electric woks of various sizes and types are availables. They have the advantage of maintaining whatever temperatures you select, especially for steaming and deep-frying foods. For making a sauce, the electric wok with a nonstick surface is convenient.

WOK WITH TWO HANDLES

This round or flat-bottomed wok has two handles, but usually one of them is long. This makes it easy to move the wok quickly over high heat with one hand while you add new ingredients. This type of the wok is especially helpful for steaming and deep-frying.

The great value of the wok is that it cooks foods quickly, retain natural juices, fresh tastes, and crispness.

The most functional size is the 14-inch(35cm) round wok.

The wok comes in various sizes, but the most functional for our purpose is the 14 inch(35cm) round wok. It is usually accompanied by a ventilated ring which serve to support the base

of the wok above a gas or an electric range-burner. Also it's fitted with a lid and an inner rack so you can steam vegetables and fish in it.

Flat-bottomed wok & Round-bottomed wok

A flat-bottomed wok does not require a ring stand. It sits directly atop the electric and element and requires some adjustments during cooking as there is direct contact with the burner, resulting in much hotter temperatures. When using a gas range, the ring should be situated with the sides slanting downwards and the smaller opening supporting the wok. The round-bottom design of the wok directs the heat source to the center of the wok which gets very hot quickly.

The heat is then conducted rapidly and evenly throughout the rest of the wok. When using an electric range, the ring should placed securely over the burner, with the sides slanting upwards to allow the center of the wok closer proximity to the burner.

SEASONING YOUR WOK

A newly purchased wok should be given special seasoning.

1.To remove the protective oil applied when manufactured, heat the wok until it begins to form a light haze.

2.Then fill it with water until almost full and bring to a boil. Discard the boiling water. Fill it with sudsy water and scrub. Rinse. Repeat 2-3 times.

3.Dry thoroughly. Then pour the oil down against the side of the wok and heat the oil over medium heat for several minutes.

4.Add some vegetable scraps and sauté, rotating the wok to coat oil around sloping sides until vegetable scraps are almost burned black. Discard the vegetable scraps and oil. Wash the wok with hot water and clean and dry thoroughly.

WOK CARE & CLEANING

1.During the course of cooking a meal, the wok need only be cleaned with hot water, using a bristle scrub brush used for non-stick pans. Never scour your wok with harsh cleansers. When you are through using the wok, wash in sudsy water and rinse.

2.Dry over medium heat and rub a dab of oil on the inside surface to prevent rust. Eventually, with constant use, your wok will assume a darker color on the inside which results in smooth non-stick cooking. If rust appears, simply scrub clean and reseason. Any time the wok is used for steaming, it must be reseasoned afterward in order to prevent foods from sticking. However, only one coating of oil is necessary for reseasoning your wok.

TO MAKE YOUR WOK COOKING FAST AND EASY:

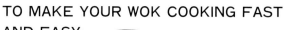

Too many ingredients in the wok can not be achieved for proper stir-frying, for instance, resulting in foods turning out soggy instead of crispy. The more ingredients in your wok, the more slowly they cook. So, in most stir-frying, we add ingredients one at a time, and push each cooked ingredients up onto the side of the wok before we add the next.

Tomiteru Shu

Born in 1950 in Yokohama, Japan, the son of Chinese parents, Tomiteru Shu has lived his whole life in Yokohama, a mecca for fans of Chinese cuisine. When he was 19, he began his training as a cook at Seikoen on Bashamichi Street, owned by his father. He currently works on the main restaurant and the annex as owner chef. He says, "Even if I create a hundred new recipes, only three will be good enough to serve to the guests." Even still he continues to work on new recipes. Now being a star chef who often appears on the TV programs and magazines, Tomiteru never hesitates talking to his customers at his restaurants. Tomitoku Shu, another popular chef is his elder brother.

Seikoen

Known for its Cantonese cuisine including fried noodles with abundant seafood; meat and seafood dishes focusing on a variety of vegetables; and dim sum dishes.

Located on historical Bashamichi, or Horse and Carriage Street, the two restaurants are so popular that people wait in line at lunch or dinner time. It is recommended that groups make reservations either for a table or a tatami room.

Main Restaurant: 5-80, Aioi-cho, Naka-ku, Yokohama. Phone:045-651-5152

Open daily from 11:30 am to 9:30 pm(8:30 pm on Holidays)

Annex Restaurant: 5-68, Ota-cho, Naka-ku, Yokohama. Phone:045-681-4121

Open daily from 11:30 am to 9:30 pm (8:30 pm on Holidays)

EASY CHINESE

APPETIZERS AND FAMILY DISHES

Cooking Assistants: Hideo Iwasa, Fujio Yojima (Seikoen Annex)

Photographers: Fumiko Sugawara, Kazuhiro Honmoto

Cover design: Sachiko Matsumura

Text Layout: Matsumura Design Office

Illustrator: Yumiko Chiba

Text: Yoshie Miura

Project editor: Kazuo Mizutani

Translator: Yoko Ishiguro